T0272627

LEADING WHAT MATTERS MOST

PHIL GELDART

LEADING WHAT MATTERS MOST

A BUSINESS PARABLE ON UNLOCKING HUMAN POTENTIAL

Forbes | Books

Published by Forbes Books, Charleston, South Carolina.
An imprint of Advantage Media Group.

Forbes Books is a registered trademark, and the Forbes Books colophon is a trademark of Forbes Media, LLC.

Printed in the United States of America.

10 9 8 7 6 5 4 3 2 1

ISBN: 979-8-88750-247-2 (Hardcover)
ISBN: 979-8-88750-248-9 (eBook)

Library of Congress Control Number: 2024904564

Cover design by Analisa Smith.
Layout design by Ruthie Wood.

Since 1917, Forbes has remained steadfast in its mission to serve as the defining voice of entrepreneurial capitalism. Forbes Books, launched in 2016 through a partnership with Advantage Media, furthers that aim by helping business and thought leaders bring their stories, passion, and knowledge to the forefront in custom books. Opinions expressed by Forbes Books authors are their own. To be considered for publication, please visit books.Forbes.com.

To Roz, my amazing wife, who has provided her unwavering love and support on our journey through life together for what is now nearly fifty years.

CONTENTS

INTRODUCTION

Very often, we as leaders receive great advice about what to do but not how to do it, and knowing the "what" without the "how" is rarely as helpful as we hoped it would be!

With that in mind, I thought I'd introduce you to Bridget, my fictional CEO running a large and highly successful tech company that is now encountering problems on the people side. While Bridget is brilliant as an operational executive, her expertise with truly releasing all the potential within her workforce is seriously lacking. This has led to declining results in both performance and employee engagement. Her board is unhappy, her people are disengaged, and her leadership team is no more people savvy than she is.

By taking Bridget's journey with her, we share in her frustrations and problems as well as her successes. More importantly, we see *how* she tackles, and ultimately resolves, these issues to the benefit of everyone involved.

You may perhaps identify with some of Bridget's challenges and be looking for insight about how to tackle them. As you follow her progress, you learn with her the practicalities of how, with the right help, you can change behaviors to improve performance.

It is my hope that you will also gain greater clarity around how you can achieve those same results ... and that Bridget's journey inspires you to truly release the potential of your own workforce!

Phil Geldart

CEO, Eagle's Flight

IT'S NO LONGER WORKING

ridget let the binders filled with financial reports and project timelines tumble out of her arms and onto her desk. Then she plopped herself into her chair. Staring at the pile, she touched a bead on her bracelet. *I wish I could make all this go away with a touch of a button as easily as I can do this*, she thought as she tapped the side of the bead and listened to the whir of her window blinds opening. She swiveled her chair around for what she knew would be a much better view. Gone were Talon Tech's faltering financial reports, the technology projections filled with a promise she may never realize, and that glaring GCG consulting report. In their place was the sparkling reflection of the sun in the slow-moving waters of the river below.

She took a deep breath and slowly exhaled. The river always had a calming effect on her, but today the sensation lasted mere seconds. The board meeting had been brutal. How had things changed so drastically in what seemed like a few short months? *We're a multibillion-dollar company with a product that people love, and we're on the brink of a new technology that will catapult us beyond any potential competitors,* she thought. *How did this happen?* Bridget hoped it wasn't too late to set things right.

Turning back to her desk, she picked up the GCG report, once again scanning the list of deficiencies. "Underdeveloped staff, low employee engagement, poor leadership competence, and ineffective corporate communication," she whispered to herself. She had dragged her heels getting this report—tried to deny the need for it, thinking she still had it under control, but she knew the board was right. Something was no longer working. Their growth was beginning to plateau, and it had nothing to do with the quality of their product or their distribution systems. She couldn't even pin it on a competitor. Talon Tech was so technologically advanced that competitors weren't even in their rearview mirror.

It felt like a sink-or-swim moment for her personally and professionally. In fact, the board chair had made that clear. Waving the GCG report, she had said, "Bridget, it took you three months to produce this report. Now you have three months to put these recommendations into action. If you can't show progress in getting these numbers turned around, we'll be forced to consider other options."

"I'll turn it around, Eliz. You can bet on it," Bridget had replied with more confidence than she felt. *I've put too much blood, sweat, and tears into this company*, Bridget thought, *I can't let it all be for nothing*.

"Bridget?"

Bridget jumped at the sound of her name and looked up.

"Looks like you were far, far away," said her assistant, Nick, with a smile. "I just wanted to let you know that it's five fifteen. I know you were trying to get home by six. I'm heading out and will see you in the morning."

"Okay. Thanks, Nick. Have a good night."

Bridget began packing up, and just before turning off her desk lamp, she decided to leave her briefcase behind. *No paperwork tonight*, she thought. And with a tap to her bracelet, she turned off the lights and locked the door.

The kids and Rob had been ready to go when she walked in the door. They had been waiting all week to see the latest Galaxy movie and had allotted her five minutes to change her clothes before they were all in the car, buckled up, and ready to go. A night out had been just what they all needed. Imaginations ignited and bellies filled with pizza and popcorn, they arrived back home with two sleepy kids in the back seat who were more than happy to go straight to bed. Exhausted herself, Bridget sat down and put her feet up for the first time all day. She reached for the glass of wine Rob offered her and let herself meld into the soft, well-worn leather of the sofa.

"Tell me all about it," Rob said. Bridget recounted the board meeting, ending with Eliz's ultimatum. "Wow, that sounds rough."

"The truth is, they're not wrong," Bridget said. "Talon Tech does have a significant problem, and a big part of it is me."

"What do you mean? Talon Tech is number one in wearable technology because of you. You provide a quality product that consumers can't get enough of. You've opened three international offices in three years—that's success if you ask me," said Rob.

Bridget smiled. "I appreciate you coming to my defense, and yes, all those things are true, but the signs are clear that we can't sustain those results doing it the same way we've been doing it—and definitely not now that we've moved into the global market. When the board sees profits and productivity trending down, customer feedback telling us our response time is too slow, and employee survey data showing concerns around leadership, morale, and commitment—

there's no hiding that there's a problem, and all those issues lead back to the CEO."

"But—" began Rob.

Bridget put her hand up to stop him, took another sip of her wine, and said, "Poor leadership was at the top of the list of deficiencies. It doesn't get more damning than that."

"Ouch," said Rob. "So, what's your plan?"

"I started with GCG, which is one of the world's largest consulting companies, asking for some direction on how to best move forward with their recommendations and if they had someone who could work with me. That was a dead end. It turns out their services effectively end when they hand over their report, so it looks like I'm flying solo. But I have my ELO mastermind group next week, and I'm sure there's a few of them who can offer me some direction. In the meantime, I'm going to meet one on one with my executives and do some fact finding on where and how things began to unravel."

As Bridget began to review department reports in preparation for her meetings with her senior team, patterns began to emerge. Talon Tech had been churning through top talent at an alarming rate for the past several years. She remembered how excited each one of them had been when they were first hired, how brilliantly they worked to execute a project, often working long nights and weekends. Now, when she took a moment to think about when and why they left, she realized it was always after a milestone had been reached—and sometimes even before that—and before the inevitable push for the next one occurred. This was where leadership had repeatedly failed, because they, herself included, were so focused on identifying the next technological feat that they didn't think about the people and what kept them engaged, motivated, and able to consistently contribute to their full potential.

Compounding these issues was the push for companies to provide more and more remote work. Originally Bridget had welcomed the idea, but now she could see the negative impact it was having on team cohesion and the informal collaboration that had allowed frustrations to be easily resolved in the natural course of the workday. She began to wrestle with the contradictory satisfaction data. The data clearly showed that her employees valued the flexibility, but her gut was telling her that the lack of human connection to each other and the company was a key element of the challenge they faced.

The more she dug into the data, the more she realized that her top team was performing below its potential, and she suspected other teams were the same and that their underperformance was due to weak leadership and a poor people-centric culture. Bridget intended to make these new insights the focus of her one-on-one meetings with her directors. That would be her opportunity to really probe into where the lines of communication and efficiencies were weakest and why.

When Bridget arrived at her ELO meeting the following week, she felt a bit embarrassed to share the challenges Talon Tech was up against. Well, not so much the challenges themselves but that she was the reason they existed. But these were a group of supportive peers, she reminded herself, who had gone through their own challenges and had a wealth of knowledge and experience they were willing to share. She presented her situation to her colleagues and shared some of the ideas she and her leadership team had to get them back on track. They lauded her for her initial efforts and offered insights. Her colleague Natasha, the CEO of a major medical equipment manufacturer, offered to send over the strategy plan her organization was employing for the transformation they began six months ago. That bolstered Bridget's confidence a bit more. As she walked to her car after the meeting, Natasha called for her to wait up.

"You look a little better than when you first walked into the meeting," Natasha said with a smile.

"I'm trying to get over my feelings of regret for not acting sooner so I can focus on the path ahead. Talking with all of you helped me cross that bridge. And thanks so much for offering to send over your strategy plan—I appreciate it," Bridget said.

"Of course," said Natasha. "Four months into our transformation, we are already producing promising results. The work we are doing with our transformation consultant is working. I'll send along his contact information with our strategy plan. I hope you can pull pieces of it that will work for Talon Tech."

"You and me both," said Bridget, turning her car on with a tap to a bead on her bracelet. "It was great seeing you, and I'm sure we'll talk soon."

The next two weeks were a blur as Bridget and her leadership team hunkered down, creating and implementing new policies and strategies for employee engagement and communication based on GCG's recommendations.

They began by addressing compensation and hiring practices with biannual bonuses based on performance and directed managers to involve team members when interviewing potential new hires. They also provided every department with a detailed outline of how to streamline processes to improve communication and increase efficiency. They knew adjustments would need to be made as the new directives were implemented, but Bridget felt it was a solid start in the right direction. She felt she had room to breathe again.

Just then her phone buzzed with a text from Marty, a colleague with years of experience as the CEO of a Fortune 500 hotel conglomerate, asking her if she was free for golf on Saturday.

"Perfect," Bridget replied.

As Bridget slid her nine iron back into her bag, she realized she had thought about little else than Talon Tech since she walked onto the course. She had hoped golf would provide her mind with a reprieve, but it didn't look like that was going to happen. "Marty," she said as they climbed into the golf cart and headed for the next hole, "can I bend your ear for a bit?"

Bridget gave Marty a quick overview of what was going on and the hope she had for the new strategies they had implemented.

"Sounds promising," said Marty, tightening his grip on the front bar as the cart bumped along the path. "Who are you working with?"

"My leadership team," said Bridget as she slowed the cart and parked it a few yards ahead of the fifth hole.

"No, I mean who are you working with outside of Talon Tech?" asked Marty.

"No one. We're working off the recommendations from GCG."

"Ah," said Marty.

"What does that mean?" said Bridget with a laugh.

"My advice," said Marty, "is to bring in an outside consultant to work through the process with you."

"We already spent three months doing that with GCG, and we're working off their recommendations."

"Suit yourself," said Marty as his club cut through the air, hitting the ball at an angle that sent it soaring. "Dang it, why can't I ever keep my shot straight on this fairway?" Turning to Bridget, he said, "You have to do what you think is best. But given the pressure from your board for fast results, you need a true transformation practitioner to walk you and the team through this. You can't afford to learn from too many mistakes as you implement this, and I know just the guy for you."

"I'm not sure we need to go that route, but send me his contact info, just in case."

Almost six weeks into the new initiatives, Bridget's leadership team continued to report grumblings from their direct reports. Sales continued to push back, saying the way they had been doing things was working fine—the company just needed to figure out how to fill their orders faster. Operations complained that they didn't have time to implement these new procedures and keep up their current production levels. Customer service grumbled about customer complaints taking up too much of their time, which meant they couldn't keep up with new orders. Why couldn't leadership work on fixing those issues instead of throwing them a measly $200 bonus, and since when was it their job to interview people? Bridget wanted to scream, but before she could, her phone rang. It was Eliz.

"Good morning, Eliz. How are you?"

"I'm good, Bridget. The real question is how are you, and how do the numbers look? There's only seven weeks until end of quarter. I hope you'll have good news for us then."

By the time Bridget fumbled her way through the call and hung up, any hopes she had built up in the past few weeks had vanished. She pulled up Talon Tech's latest earnings report she had been working on. *No, Eliz, I don't have good news*, she thought. But here she was. She'd have to provide the board with a report. *And then what?* she thought. *Beg them to give me another quarter to not make any progress?*

Wait, thought Bridget. *Maybe Marty's given me the Hail Mary I need.* Looking more closely at the card, she recognized the name as the same consultant she'd seen on the file Natasha had sent over a couple of months ago.

She couldn't dial the number he'd given her fast enough.

"Hello, this is Ray Ortiz. How can I help you?"

MOVING FROM
WHAT TO HOW

"   s this table all right?" asked the hostess, ushering Bridget to a small table in the center of the bustling restaurant.

"Actually," said Bridget looking around the room, "could we have one of the booths in the corner over there? It looks a bit quieter."

"Certainly, and how many in your party?"

"I'm expecting one guest, Ray Ortiz. If you could direct him here when he arrives, that would be great," said Bridget as she slid into the booth.

"Of course," said the hostess, handing Bridget the wine list. "Your server will be right with you."

Bridget took off her jacket and folded it neatly beside her before scanning the list. As she debated between merlot and pinot noir, her phone buzzed. She answered it. "Hi, hon—I'm just about to start my meeting. What's up?"

"This will be quick," promised Rob. "Maddie just wanted to say good night to you." Bridget loved that Maddie still wanted to do this. Their son, Craig, now eleven, was no longer so enamored with her except on rare occasions.

"Hi, Mommy."

"Hi, Maddie Bear—you ready for bed?"

"Yup. Good night, Mommy. I love you."

"Good night, sweetie. I love you, too."

"See, I told you it would be quick," said Rob with a laugh. "Good luck with your meeting—can't wait to hear all about it."

"Bridget?"

Bridget looked up to see Ray approaching the table. "Gotta go," she whispered into the phone and ended the call. "Ray? It's so nice to meet you."

"Please don't get up," he said, putting his hand up and sliding into the seat across from her.

They talked about the weather and what looked good on the menu. After placing their order, the conversation moved on to family and where they were from. With their salads now in front of them, Bridget decided it was time to jump in.

"I'm guessing the first order of business is telling you all that's going wrong with Talon Tech so you can fix it."

Ray laughed. "Well, you have that partly right. I do need to know what prompted you to call me, but I'm not going to fix the problem."

Bridget's fork paused in midair. "If you're not going to fix it, why are we here?"

"I'm going to *show* you how you and your team can achieve the results you're looking for and then be there to help you and them on that journey," said Ray.

"And how do you intend to do that?" asked Bridget.

"I promise I'll explain in detail, but first I need to understand what you are trying to accomplish at Talon Tech."

"Well, I'm happy with the business. I'm happy with our customers. I'm happy with our product."

"Maybe I'm the one who should be asking why we're here," Ray said with a smile. "Sorry for the interruption—please continue."

"The truth is, as recently as a week ago I was still resistant to taking this step. I think because Talon Tech has done so well—we're at the top of our industry, and we continue, at least until now, to turn a healthy profit—it's blinded me to some very real issues. Issues that I should have addressed sooner, but now, months after there were initial indications of potential trouble, I'm finally taking the steps that I hope will help me right the ship before it's too late."

Ray leaned forward. "You have my full attention. Tell me everything, starting from the initial indications to all the steps you've taken up to today."

Bridget barely touched her salad, trying to bring Ray up to speed. As she shared the details, Ray interjected now and then with questions that made her walk around the entire problem and realize that she couldn't approach this like a glitch in a piece of technology. A 360-degree view of Talon Tech—its strengths, weaknesses, and, most importantly, why those weaknesses existed and the fallout if she didn't figure out a way to fix it—was beginning to come into focus.

Before she could formulate her next thought, Ray said, "I think what's happened is you don't know how to harness the potential of your workforce. You and your leaders know how to lead the business, but you don't know how to effectively lead your people."

Bridget felt validated. Ray had just confirmed what she had begun to suspect was the root cause of Talon Tech's problem. She was not a people person, and she was realizing the significance of the disadvantage she had let that create. "You're right, Ray. I feel that neither I nor my leaders are equipped to adjust to the evolving landscapes of how our people work and what they need. Optimizing how people contribute is not my strong suit, so how in the world can I get my leaders to do it if I can't?"

"One step at a time," Ray assured her. "I'll walk you through the how and answer all your questions. But first, I need you to answer a question for me. Are you willing to do what it takes to get the outcomes you want?"

"Of course!" said Bridget, reaching for a warm roll and a scoop of butter.

"Okay," said Ray. "I can see that you are highly motivated. What I need to know," he continued, "is how committed are you?"

"One hundred percent," said Bridget confidently.

"One hundred percent committed looks different for everyone," said Ray. "When you say one hundred percent, does that mean, let's say, in a bacon-and-egg breakfast, that you have the commitment of the chicken or the pig or somewhere in between?"

Bridget's eyes narrowed. "Do I have the commitment of a what?"

"Let me say that another way. In a bacon-and-egg breakfast, what's the difference in the level of commitment between the chicken and the pig?"

Bridget paused for a moment. "The chicken can still cluck after breakfast!"

"Exactly. The pig is committed, but the chicken is merely involved. If you're expecting to write me a check, hoping the problem will go away, then you're not really committed. You're involved and you care, but you're not committed. As you know, Bridget, *commitment* at the CEO level is typically manifested by providing resources, like money and staff, and then giving them to a senior VP and telling them to get on with it. That's involvement and impactful, but it doesn't actually require you to do real work."

"You've asked me if I think like a pig or a chicken, and now you tell me I don't do real work. You do want me to hire you, right?" Bridget said with a grin.

"Chicken marsala for you, ma'am, and shrimp scampi for you, sir," said their server as he placed their meals in front of them. *How appropriate*, thought Bridget.

"Thank you,'" Bridget and Ray said in unison as they pushed their salad and bread plates aside to make room.

"I'll take those out of your way," said the server, scooping up the now unnecessary plates and utensils.

Spearing one of his shrimps with his fork, Ray said, "Where were we?"

"I think you were telling me I don't do real work," said Bridget.

"Ah, yes," laughed Ray. "What I mean is that your real work is in other areas. You meet other CEOs, you meet with senior customers, you chair meetings, you lay out visions and strategies, but you aren't involved with the tasks that get the job done. But if you're going to lead differently and you're going to ask people to change the way they behave, then you are going to have to do some things differently— you're going to have to change the way *you* behave with regard to your people management."

"I'm a little confused. My focus is making the necessary changes to Talon Tech, not me."

"That's true. But it's also true that if you want your organization to change, *you* must change. If you don't want your organization to change, you don't have to change at all. But the body follows the head. So, if you don't change, your leadership and employees aren't going to change—and if they don't change, neither does your organization."

"Okay," she said. "I get that. Now, what exactly do you mean by changing *my* behavior?"

"The first change is less about the amount of time that you spend on this and more about the priority that you make it. Let me give you an example. As soon as we begin this initiative, you'll need to reference it in your regular meetings with your staff, in your town halls, and in employee objectives and reviews," explained Ray.

"Okay. So, it's basically treating it like any other important thing that I want people to do, like supporting a new acquisition."

"Correct."

"That makes sense. It's a matter of making this initiative a priority," said Bridget.

"Exactly. I just need to know what priority it is for you."

"Oh, it's definitely number one," said Bridget.

"Okay," said Ray with a hint of a question in his voice. "Just to be clear, you are saying this initiative is your number one priority, which means there are no other priorities that supersede this?"

"Well, of course I have other priorities. But this will be one of my top priorities."

"I understand it will be one of your top priorities, Bridget, and it's okay if this initiative isn't the number one priority. I just need to know where it truly sits on Talon Tech's and your priority list. What number is it?"

"How is everything?" asked their server as he topped off their water glasses. "Can I get you anything?"

"Thank you," said Ray. "I'm all set for now."

"Ma'am?" The server turned to Bridget.

"Yes?" asked Bridget.

"Can I get you anything?"

"Oh, sorry," said Bridget, still sorting out her thoughts on what priority this initiative needed to be. "I'm good, thank you."

Bridget looked at Ray. "It will be priority number three. Priority one is product quality, and priority two is making our sales for the year."

"Great. Now I know that if it falls below three on your priority list, you and I are going to have a conversation."

"Okay," she said. "Absolutely."

"Because I am going to let everyone in the organization know this is the number three priority, and that number one is product quality and number two is to meet sales numbers for the year."

"Why does it matter whether everyone knows my priorities?"

"Because," said Ray, "you need to let them know from the beginning what your level of commitment to this initiative is. Then if something happens that requires all hands on deck for priority number one or two and your team sees you take the company's focus off this initiative during that period, people won't wonder if this initiative was a passing fad and you're not committed to it. They'll understand that it's a temporary pause to deal with a higher priority, but we're going to get back to it as soon as possible.

"This initiative doesn't have to be all consuming. In fact, it's not changing *what* you do or how Talon Tech operates, but *how* you lead and manage the people who are getting the work done." Ray paused and then continued. "But you need to understand that if you decide to go down this path, you can't delegate it, procrastinate it, or ignore it. You must put it in its proper perspective and lead it. Your personal behavior must result in truly releasing the potential of your workforce.

And by the way, once these new behaviors are in place throughout the entire company, it doesn't just address your current concerns but also contributes significantly to improving other areas like quality and safety."

Bridget took a deep breath. "Wow! Okay, so in practice, what do you need me to do?"

"Great question, Bridget, and definitely the right next question," said Ray. As they finished up their main course, Ray explained that Bridget would need to cascade her level of commitment to all her direct reports by letting them know that this was a priority and holding them accountable to execute it.

"You must let them know that their commitment and involvement is nonnegotiable. You must tell them, 'This is something that we must do and are going to do. If you don't want to sign on for this, that's fine. I absolutely understand and respect that. But if that's the case, Talon Tech isn't going to be the place for you.'"

"What!" Bridget exclaimed, nearly knocking over her water glass as she tried to contain her surprise. "I can't just tell them, 'Get on board today or get out.' What if they all get out? Having my leadership walk out will *not* solve my problem."

"You're right, Bridget. But having a team member who is not fully committed to this initiative will guarantee failure, since everyone in the entire organization ultimately reports to someone in that room. However, if they do sign on, it will be my job to ensure that each one of them is successful, and we'll tell them that."

"But …"

As the conversation continued, Bridget was relieved to hear Ray explain that in his experience, typically no one leaves initially, and often no one leaves at all. He reiterated that regardless, it was imperative that Bridget unequivocally state that this was not a debatable point and that anyone who wasn't committed to this direction could come see her and exit with a great package. He went on to explain how the cascading of both her and their commitment to the initiative must flow to everyone in the organization responsible for people. Her leadership team would need to make it clear to their own direct reports that the initiative was a priority and hold them accountable for it, and they in turn would then need to do the same with their direct reports, and so on down the line.

"Bridget, I need you to make sure that every leader in this company embraces and leads this initiative. Are you willing to put in place what is necessary to make that happen?"

Bridget paused, letting herself be mesmerized by the wine as she swirled it around in her glass. The prospect of what Ray was suggesting was suddenly terrifying. How had she not considered that she could lose people in this process? The fallout from that … she tried not to think of it. If she was honest with herself, she wasn't 100 percent confident she had what it would take to stay the course. She looked at Ray, who was patiently waiting for an answer, and realized that what was even more terrifying was the fallout if she *didn't* take this step. She set her glass down, and the swirling wine grew still.

"Yes, I'm willing to make it happen."

"Good," said Ray. "Now, the next hurdle. If you are serious about moving forward, do you have the budget to do it? Because it's going to cost you money. In my experience, your investment will be paid back many times, and we can chat about the payback if you want, but you will need the budget, and my team and I will need access to the leaders and their staff."

Bridget agreed that she could find the budget. Now what she wanted to know was how that budget would be spent.

"It's going to require an investment in time as well as money," Ray explained, "because my team and I are going to have to train every leader in this company, including you, on the new behaviors and then provide consistent follow-up as they put those new behaviors into practice. Because changing behaviors takes time, there will be more time spent on the follow-up and ongoing support with application back on the job than on training itself."

"So, you train the leaders, and then what? We go tell everyone how and what to do?"

"Not exactly. We'll teach them the new behaviors and show how to apply them through modeling, coaching, and requiring the behaviors. But before we get ahead of ourselves, once the leaders know how to lead in a way that harnesses the potential of their teams and their people, we'll also need to train all the employees on the new behaviors, too."

Bridget was quiet.

"Questions?" asked Ray.

"Oh yes." Bridget smiled, her eyes wide. "Lots of questions." Bridget motioned for their server. Handing him the empty breadbasket, she asked, "Could we get a refill on these, please? They were delicious."

"Absolutely," said the server, reaching for the basket. "No one can resist our rolls," he said with a wink.

"Training," sighed Bridget. "The mention of the word sends everyone running. Training often feels like we are throwing time and money away because most people either don't take in the information, or if they do, they apply it for a week or two and then forget about it—that's if they even show up for the training. There's an abundance of training options out there that require a lot less time and money than what you are suggesting."

"I'm sure there are. 'Typical' training, as you said, provides information in the hope that people will take it in and apply it. We're not typical, and we don't throw a bunch of information out and hope it sticks. Using our experiential learning approach, your employees will learn by doing, and then over the next two years we'll provide them the support needed to keep on doing it until it becomes habitual. However, you'll begin to see meaningful results very quickly. It's ensuring those results are sustained that takes the time."

"Wow! You weren't kidding when you said it would require significant commitment—I'll be honest, two years is a bit intimidating, but it also makes sense given the depth of transformation I think we are talking about. It's also reassuring to know that we don't have to wait two years to see results."

"Coming to grips with the total time required is a common response," Ray assured her. "Comprehending the level of commitment required to achieve the outcomes you want year after year, and even beyond your tenure with Talon Tech, is a process. It's critical that you stay with it until it's part of the organization's culture. The intent is to continue to see its impact long after you've left. It's also critical that you understand how challenging keeping that commitment will be sometimes."

Bridget felt a bit like she was on a roller-coaster ride—one moment full of confidence this was the right path for Talon Tech, and then moments like this, when she struggled to wrap her head around the entirety of the initiative. "Challenging in what other ways?" she asked, placing her palms flat on the table as if to brace for impact.

"This is a tough one," cautioned Ray, "but among the imperatives for this to be successful is that no one is allowed to opt out of the training. No one. Your commitment as the leader is to guarantee that this initiative is a high enough priority that everyone attends their scheduled training sessions. Can you commit to doing that?"

Bridget imagined the ensuing battle with manufacturing when she told them this and, even tougher, the challenge of explaining to the board how doing so would set Talon Tech on a stronger financial course. "Before I can answer that, I need you to be straight with me." Bridget leaned in, holding Ray's gaze. "Will your training and experiential approach really work, Ray? Will you guarantee we will continue to get the outcomes over the long haul?"

"Our doing the training will not make it work. Your people consistently applying what we've taught you in the training will make it work—and remember, we will be alongside you the whole time to keep you on this journey. By training your people, aligning Talon Tech's leaders, and providing the right tools, you will have everything you need to achieve your desired outcomes as long as you apply the teaching until the new behaviors become habitual. If you and your leaders apply what we teach you to do, I guarantee it will work."

It was only as she exhaled that Bridget realized she had been holding her breath during Ray's answer. Finally, she felt like she was on a straightaway and could begin to see a path forward. It was becoming clear that this level of disciplined process technique was different from anything she had experienced before. The series of steps Ray would be guiding them through gave her confidence.

"I'm wholly committed to Talon Tech," said Bridget. "I've worked long and hard to get us where we are, and we haven't even scratched the surface of what we could be. I intend to lead Talon Tech to its full potential. The process you've laid out is logical—if I lead it, you show us what to do, we do it, and everyone practices it, it will be successful. But why 'everyone' right from the start? Why don't we just start with a small group or pilot location? Then, once everyone sees it's working, we could roll it out."

"There are two reasons," explained Ray. "First, a start-small approach sends the message that you're not fully committed to doing all that's required but instead are just going to 'give it a try.' That level of commitment will not ensure success."

"And the second?" asked Bridget.

"Your organization, like all others, runs on processes and steps taken by individuals or teams that are all interconnected. Work always flows from one group to another. If you initially train only a portion of the company, when those who are engaging in the new behaviors interact with those who have not been trained, conflicting behaviors, approaches, and expectations occur, and you end up worse off than when you started."

"I get it. My answer is yes, *everyone* will attend all trainings— no exceptions."

"I believe you can do this, Bridget, and if you do, I know Talon Tech will achieve the future you envision."

"I'm on board," she said, setting her now empty plate to the side, "but I still have questions."

"Of course—fire away," said Ray.

"You've talked a lot about training our leaders to be better leaders. Can you give me an example of what that looks like?"

"Sure. Right now, your leaders are making decisions based on feedback from a couple of people. What would happen if we trained them to gather input from all the people who will be implementing that decision?"

"Well, that would be a better way, because the people who have to implement it are the ones who best know the implications," said Bridget.

"Exactly. We'll provide your people with a model in which they gather input from everyone who will be affected before they make their decision. The common response we get from leaders is, 'Do I have to accept all that input?' And the answer is no. We will also provide them with tools to determine which input to accept and which to reject, and we'll show them how to ensure the people whose input they did not accept still feel valued. But the decision process doesn't end there."

"But the decision in your scenario has been made to move forward using this new process," said Bridget. "Now, people just need to implement it."

"True," said Ray. "But the leader still needs to make sure that the employees implementing it have the tools and resources to make that happen and that they feel confident they can do the job. If they don't, a 'good' decision can't be, or doesn't, get implemented. Addressing that requires another set of skills and tools. Put together, this approach enables your leaders to make better decisions with guaranteed results."

"That would be amazing," agreed Bridget. "I can see how that would require a significant behavior change to move from our current process of 'Here's the decision—go implement it' to 'I value your input and want to hear what you have to say before I make the decision.' And … then really listening and acting on that input. That's an awfully big gap to close in a few days of training. The need for a two-year commitment is beginning to make sense to me now."

"It is a big gap to close, and you're right, no one is going to learn everything they need to know and how to put it into practice in a day or two or even over a few months. That's why every three months we'll bring back your leaders and give them an opportunity to ask questions about the application of the model. We want to know how they feel it's going. What's working and what isn't working for them. We'll walk your leaders through every scenario that challenged them over the past three months and guide them through it. And this decision model is just one of the new skills we'll equip them with."

Ray could see Bridget needed a few moments to digest all the information he had just shared. "How about I order us some coffee and desserts? I noticed your eyes lit up when our server listed chocolate layer cake as one of the favorites on the dessert menu. Should I order that for you?"

"That would be great," said Bridget as she pulled out her phone and began typing. She needed to get her initial thoughts down and put them in some sort of order. This exercise always helped her better see the big picture, and given the level of commitment Ray was talking about, she needed clarity on the impact of this investment from a thirty-thousand-foot view.

"Chocolate cake and decaf for you, ma'am, and lemon meringue pie and tea for you, sir," said their server as he placed the items on the table.

"Thank you," said Ray. "Looks delicious."

"Thank you," said Bridget, looking up from her notes for a moment. She then looked at Ray. "Please go ahead," she said, gesturing to his slice of pie. "I just need one more moment to finish my train of thought."

"Of course," said Ray, happily guiding his fork through the fluffy meringue and into the dense lemon filling, finally scooping it all up in the cradle of the light, flaky crust.

When Bridget next looked up, Ray's plate was empty but for a few stray crumbs. "I hope my dessert is as good as yours apparently was," laughed Bridget.

"You should be so lucky," said Ray, relaxing into the back of his seat. "So," he said, pointing to her phone, "I'm guessing you have more questions."

"Just one," said Bridget. "When can we get started?"

On the drive home, Bridget mentally reviewed her conversation with Ray and all it implied for not only Talon Tech's future but her own future as a leading technology CEO. By the time she pulled into the garage and turned off the engine, her thoughts were becoming more structured, and she was anxious to sort them out.

"How'd the meeting go … and what are you looking for?" asked Rob as he watched his wife rummage through her desk drawers.

"It was a bit terrifying," Bridget said. "Ah, here it is." She smiled as she pulled a leather-bound notebook from beneath the files in her bottom drawer. "But also exhilarating," she said, looking up at her husband as he leaned against the open door of her study.

"Sounds interesting," said Rob. "What's the notebook for?"

"This," said Bridget, holding it up like a gauntlet, "is my new Transformation Notebook!"

"Really?" said Rob. "I can't remember the last time you wrote anything down with a pen and paper," he said, laughing.

"I know, I know," said Bridget, "and maybe it's silly, but I need to start looking at things in new ways, and maybe putting my thoughts and ideas about Talon Tech's transformation on paper will help me start doing just that."

Bridget gave Rob a quick overview of the key points from her conversation with Ray.

"Sounds like you think it will work," said Rob.

"I really think it will," said Bridget with a gleam in her eye Rob hadn't seen in months. As Bridget sat down at her desk, she said, "I just have a few more notes to make, and then I'll be up." Rob gave her a wink and headed off to bed.

Bridget was up bright and early the next morning. Showered and dressed, she headed out to the porch with her coffee and Transformation Notebook. Setting her coffee down and settling into the overstuffed wicker chair, she reviewed her notes from the night before.

Embed a people-first culture in the fabric of the organization by doing the following:

- *Recognize that leadership behaviors and employee behaviors need to be different than they currently are. It's not about different "HR" policies and procedures.*

- *Equip all leaders to demonstrate "true" leadership that allows and encourages people to perform to their full potential.*

        □ *Encourage input into decisions.*

        □ *Provide additional new tools and skills to help them do their job brilliantly.*

- *Consistently communicate the people-first initiative to all employees. Let them know where Talon Tech is going with respect to enabling them to contribute to their full potential and their importance to our future by*

        □ *defining this priority and sticking to it,*

        □ *referencing this initiative in regular staff meetings and company-wide town halls, and*

        □ *ensuring that employee objectives and reviews reflect this initiative.*

- *Training and practice*

        □ *Lead + Train + Implement + Practice = Success.*

Bridget could feel her anxiety resurface as she reread her training and practice list. She fought the urge to add to the list:

- *Everyone in training—no exceptions could mean*

        □ *shutting down production,*

        □ *angry people, and*

        □ *people quitting*

How had she committed to everyone attending training—no excuses? What would that even look like? What if someone refused? Was she really ready to let them go if they weren't 100 percent on board with the initiative? She knew the level of commitment Ray had talked about made sense if they were to truly transform, but how realistic was that? *Everything sounds amazing in the heat of the moment,* she thought, *and now, in the light of the morning sun, the cracks are revealed.* She added the following to her notes:

- *Ask Ray how to handle scenarios when people tell me they can't make it to the training sessions.*

Remember:

- *Two-year process means staying the course despite early positive results.*

Bridget closed her journal and watched the iridescent green hummingbird flutter in and out of the lantana blossoms that surrounded the porch. "I think I need to gather from more than one blossom, too," she whispered to herself.

On her way to the office, Bridget called Natasha and Marty and set up meetings with each of them that afternoon. Before Ray and she met with her senior leadership team tomorrow morning, she hoped she could get a shot of perspective and confidence from her colleagues who, in Marty's case, had already made the transformation, and Natasha, who was currently in the thick of it.

THE LEAP
OF FAITH

"Trust the process," Bridget said softly to herself, channeling the advice both Natasha and Marty gave her yesterday. Natasha had told her that she needed to build an army of support, and that army consisted of everyone in her organization who was leading people.

"You need to help them understand what you're doing and why you're doing it," had been Natasha's final comment.

Marty had echoed similar sentiments. "You need the passion and conviction to lead this, Bridget. That's the only way you will make these changes become real in the hearts and minds of every leader and employee at Talon Tech. You are in good hands with Ray and his team; you just need to trust the process."

Her phone buzzed. She hit speaker. "Yes, Nick."

"Mr. Ortiz is here to see you."

"Thanks, Nick. Let him know I'll be right there."

The moment of truth, Bridget thought as she stepped out into reception. "Good morning, Ray. Good to see you. Welcome to Talon Tech," she said with a smile.

"Good morning, Bridget," he said, shaking her hand warmly. "I'm glad to be here and look forward to meeting your team."

"It looks like you're going to meet one of them right now." Bridget looked in the direction of the familiar sound of heels clicking on the tiled floor. "Gisela," she called, waving her over.

"Good morning, Gisela. I'd like you to meet Ray Ortiz."

"Ah," said Gisela, slipping her phone into her pocket. "The new consultant who's going to fix all our problems, right?"

Before Ray could reply, Bridget said, "Gisela is our chief revenue officer."

"Good morning, Mr. Ortiz," said Gisela.

"Please, call me Ray. Nice to meet you, Gisela."

Gisela turned to Bridget. "I'm glad I caught you before you went into the meeting. I wanted to let you know that I'm expecting—" Gisela was interrupted by the chiming of her phone. "This call." Gisela turned to Ray, "I'm sorry that I'm going to be late for our first meeting together, Ray."

"Please wait a moment," Bridget said to Gisela. She turned to Ray. "The conference room is the second door on the right. We'll be right there."

Gisela's phone continued to buzz. "Can this wait, Bridget? I really need to take this call."

Bridget looked at her watch. "The meeting starts in six minutes, Gisela. You need to be seated and ready to start by then."

"I'll do my best," said Gisela, frantically looking from Bridget to her phone.

"Gisela, you need to be seated and ready to go in the conference room no later than eleven o'clock," said Bridget. Gisela glared at her.

So, this is what commitment is going to look like, thought Bridget as she turned and began to walk down the hall. *I'll either have a heart attack or a mutiny on my hands within twenty-four hours.*

"Rachel," she heard Gisela say, "I just got a call from the Singapore office, and unfortunately I can't take the call right now. Can you please call the office, apologize for me, and schedule a call for this afternoon at a time that is convenient for them."

At 10:58 a.m., Bridget breathed a sigh of relief. All her executives were seated and ready to go.

"Good morning, everyone. Welcome to the first meeting of Talon Tech's new approach to addressing the issues you all know we face and absolutely must resolve." That raised some eyebrows, but Bridget did not let that distract her. "I'd like you all to meet Ray Ortiz, a recognized thought leader on human potential in today's business climate. Ray is the CEO of a global company specializing in leadership development, culture transformation, and—critical to us—the releasing of every individual's full potential. Ray has agreed to personally be involved with us and serve as the guiding force behind the journey we are about to embark on. But before I hand him the floor, I'd like to go around the table and have you each introduce yourself."

They spent the next fifteen minutes with introductions, each executive providing Ray a summary of what they did and their history with Talon Tech. "Thank you, everyone," Bridget said when the last person had been introduced. "Before Ray begins, I ask that you all put your phones away."

"You can't be serious," said Gisela.

"I am," said Bridget holding Gisela's gaze.

Gisela and Jordan, Talon Tech's chief manufacturing officer, exchanged looks before putting their phones away.

"It's a pleasure to meet you all," said Ray. "What you have all accomplished here at Talon Tech is incredibly impressive. The reason I'm here is that Talon Tech has been wrestling with problems. I know you have tried to identify the origin of the problems and ways to address them and that those efforts have failed. But I assure you, there is a path forward—a path that will lead to the outcomes Talon Tech needs and you all want to achieve to continue your impressive successes." Ray met everyone's eyes before continuing.

"Bridget has made it clear to me that the approach I'm about to lay out for you is the path that Talon Tech will follow. Its success requires the commitment of every leader in this room. Now, I know you don't yet understand this approach or your role in it, and I respect that, but everyone at Talon Tech must be committed to the path."

A phone buzzed. No one reached for it.

Ray continued. "Some of you will be excited about that. Others, probably the majority, are neither excited nor negative but want to know more, and some of you may have already decided against it before hearing the details. Bridget and I have had a conversation, and if you choose not to be on this path, then Talon Tech probably isn't the right place for—"

Jordan cut in. "Isn't the right place for whom? All due respect, Ray, but remember how incredibly impressive you find Talon Tech? Well," she said, extending her arm and circling it around the table, "we are the ones who helped make it incredibly impressive. Now you're telling us that anyone who doesn't agree with the new path forward—a path we had no knowledge of, let alone input on—will be fired?" She turned to Bridget. "Bridget?"

"I understand your concerns, all of you," said Bridget, "but that doesn't change the fact that we need to take significant action; action that will guarantee Talon Tech's long-term success. As CEO, this is the direction in which I will be leading Talon Tech. If, after you hear all that Ray has to say, you decide it's not a direction you wish to take, I respect that. You can come see me after the meeting, and we'll give you the best package possible." Bridget looked around the table at all the talented people who'd helped make Talon Tech what it was and hoped she wouldn't lose any of them. "I *trust* the process. If you can't do that yet, then I ask you to trust me." Bridget turned to Ray. "Please continue."

"Thank you, Bridget," Ray began again. "I want to make clear that if you are willing to be part of the change that's coming, then my goal is to ensure your success, both as individuals and as a company." Ray then provided the team an overview of the discussion he and Bridget had had a couple of days before, reviewing what they already knew were issues and what Bridget and he saw as the missing link to solving those issues: an approach to leading people that complemented the company's level of scale. If they didn't take action to address Talon Tech's disengaged workforce that was operating below their potential, it would only be a matter of time before they lost their competitive advantage.

He concluded with the following: "The goal of committing to being people centric is to release the potential and capability of every employee. The additional contribution that will generate will improve all company metrics. A people-centric culture enables every employee to contribute to their full potential and to be supported in that by their line manager. This leads to improving the critical success factors and achieving the vision of the company. I believe everyone around this table wants Talon Tech to reach its full potential—whatever that may be. To do that, I ask you to trust the process, and let's transform Talon Tech together."

Letting the silence sit for a minute, Ray reached for the pitcher at the center of the table and filled his glass with water. He took a sip. Setting his glass down, he looked around the table. "So," he said, "from everything I just said, what did you hear?"

"Lots of changes, including replacing most of us with a new leadership team. That's how these transformations generally go," said DeAngela Jones, Talon Tech's chief operating officer.

"More training," said Andrea Stiles, Talon Tech's chief information officer. "Training that eats up development time."

"Time that also eats into revenue," chimed in Gisela. "I hope this people initiative, or whatever we're calling it, won't supersede our year-end sales goals. We have enough challenges in front of us as it is, and if we can't meet our sales goals that bring in revenue to keep us running, what's the point?"

The others shared their initial thoughts, ranging from skepticism to glimmers, however slight, of excitement.

"All valid concerns," agreed Ray, "concerns that I will address with you."

Dishant, Talon Tech's chief financial officer, looked around the table at his colleagues and said, "I think you all know that Bridget's right. We need to take significant action, or we risk losing everything we've worked to build. To me, the risk of losing Talon Tech comes at a much higher cost than the risk of committing to a plan that promises to help us achieve the outcomes we all want," said Dishant. "And," he said with a nod at Bridget, "I trust Bridget."

Those three words gave Bridget a swell of confidence. *One person on my team. Everything starts with one*, she thought. Bridget wanted to take advantage of Dishant's positive note. She stood up. "I think this is a good time for a quick break while they bring lunch in." Better to have everyone talking about the risk of losing Talon

Tech if they didn't follow the new direction than moaning about training. "I need everyone back and ready to go at twelve forty-five, so be back a few minutes early if you want time to grab a sandwich to eat while we work."

Much to Bridget's surprise, Gisela and Jordan returned early, had grabbed a sandwich and drink, and were seated at the table ready to go … or perhaps, she smiled in spite of herself, they were simply conspiring to overthrow her. *The two of them certainly present some challenges*, thought Bridget, *but they're intelligent, quick to identify and resolve potential problems, and passionate about their work. I hope they are willing to get on board.*

"I'm glad to see everyone decided to return," Ray said with a chuckle when everyone was back in their seats, for which he received a few reluctant smiles. "Just before the break, some concerns had been raised. Concerns I promised to address. Let's do that before we go any further."

He turned to DeAngela. "DeAngela, you voiced concerns about replacing the leadership team. That is a common assumption in these circumstances, but I can assure you it has not been my experience, nor do I want it to be my experience." He looked around the room. "I've heard nothing but accolades about each one of you from Bridget, and I assure you it is not Bridget's or my intention to change the people sitting around this table. As Jordan pointed out, you are all the reason for Talon Tech's incredible success. We're not asking anybody to work a miracle. We are simply requiring every leader to give this initiative their full effort."

Ray looked around the table. "Let's go down this path together, and in three or four months, we'll see if it's starting to pay back."

Bridget could see shoulders relaxing and tension releasing from faces. Not by everyone, but a few. The release of stress was most obvious in Samantha Sullivan, Talon Tech's chief marketing officer. Samantha was the newest member of the team, and Bridget could imagine she was thinking exactly what Bridget would be thinking in her position: *Last one in, first one out.* She liked Samantha. She was genuine, bright, and innovative. It had been just under ten months since she had relocated her young family here from the West Coast. Bridget felt confident she would commit to what needed to be done.

Ray then turned his attention to Andrea. "Andrea, I can also understand your concerns about what a wasted drain training can be."

His honest comment surprised her and got her attention.

"Has anyone here had a really good training experience with long-term impact?" continued Ray. Just as he was about to resume the conversation, Ray saw Tyler Robinson, Talon Tech's chief legal officer, hesitantly raise his hand.

"Ha," said DeAngela, laughing. "Yes, Tyler, we all know you love training." That drew chuckles from everyone around the table.

"I can't help it," said Tyler, pretending to swat DeAngela's arm. "In my job, you can never know too much!"

Bridget was glad to see some camaraderie return to the group. Most of the time they really did work well together.

"Well, I'm certainly happy to hear there is someone who is a fan of training here," joked Ray. He, too, was glad to see some levity among the team, and he took it as an opportunity to engage them. "Let's walk through a quick scenario together. Everyone on board?" He took the three or four head nods as a yes for the group.

"If you drop a stone in a pool, you get ripples, right?" asked Ray. Everyone agreed that was true. Ray then walked them through a scenario involving an employee having an accident on the job that resulted in a serious injury. "What happens on the job?"

Everyone agreed that someone has to fill the position so the job would get done.

"What does that mean for the person who has to fill in? What if they had a family vacation planned during that time?"

Ray could see everyone's wheels turning. He knew that in this type of situation, leaders often consider it taken care of once the vacancy is filled and the workers' comp issue dealt with.

"His family is going to be pretty disappointed," said Jordan. "It's happened to me, and I still don't think my kids have forgiven me. And I can tell you, I was not my best self at work that week, thinking about how I was supposed to be on vacation."

"This is going to sound terrible," said Tyler, "but I'm focused on the legal consequences for the company. What if the guy who was injured sues us? That would be a mess I'd rather avoid."

"What about the guy who's injured and won't be able to return to work?" asked Ray, "What happens to him? What will it mean for his family?"

Everyone was quiet. "The ripple effect of one accident is significant for many people beyond the injured person and the company, isn't it?" Ray asked. Everyone nodded in agreement. "What if you could prevent the accident?"

"We'd stop the ripples," came a quiet voice. It was the first time Ray had heard Harry, Talon Tech's chief people officer, contribute to the conversation since they had all introduced themselves at the beginning of the meeting. He had seemed disengaged, and Ray had wondered if he was even listening. Clearly, he had been.

"Yes, Harry," agreed Ray. "You, and everyone around this table, have the power to stop the ripples that are coming with increasing frequency from your current situation. My team and I aren't going to tell you how—I promise there is no 'death by PowerPoint' in our training—we are going to provide you experiential learning and highly engaging training sessions that let you discover and understand new ways you can behave to achieve the outcomes you're all looking for."

From there, Ray went on to explain in detail the six areas—leadership, communication, alignment, training, reinforcement, and metrics—that Ray and his team would focus on and how they would support the leadership team with each.

"Each one of us in this room must be brilliant in the way we harness the potential of the people—how we think about our people and how we treat our people. Once we have that, we have success." He then turned to Gisela. "Gisela, I didn't forget you. Let's address your concerns about priorities."

Ray outlined Bridget's and thus Talon Tech's three top priorities. Gisela beamed when she heard that making year-end sales was a priority above this new approach. Ray went on to explain that while this initiative may, on rare occasions, be adjusted to accommodate any immediate needs to elevate focus on priorities one or two, those adjustments would always be temporary and Talon Tech's people initiative would remain one of Talon Tech's top three priorities.

"So," said Harry, "if I understand you correctly, here's what it is." And he set out the following outline:

- We have three priorities.

- We provide new behaviors at every level.

- It will be leader led.

- We'll align all our HR practices.

- We put everything you show/teach us into practice.

- You and your team provide guidance and support.

"Yes," said Ray with a smile. "That's exactly it!"

Bridget closed the door of her car and leaned her head back against the seat. She closed her eyes and took a few deep breaths. It had been a very long day. She was exhausted but also hopeful. The meeting and her team's response had ended on a more positive note than she had expected. Harry's "get it" factor and support was especially encouraging, as having HR in the boat with her would be a great asset. Equally encouraging was Dishant's understanding of the urgency and his resulting support given his role as CFO and the one who would have to find the money this would cost.

Bridget opened her windows, welcoming the cool breeze. She then pulled her Transformation Notebook from her bag and began to note her reflections of the day before heading home.

Six Areas of Focus:

- *Leadership: Each of us must own the outcome for this initiative.*

- *Communication: Let everyone know continually and consistently how we are doing things differently and why.*

- *Alignment: Align all the human resource practices.*

- *Training: Experiential training. First train leaders at all levels, then train all employees*

- *Reinforcement: Provide support and activities to ensure that the training sticks.*

- *Metrics: Continuous measurement of progress/outcomes.*

Ask Ray the following:

- *When will we start to see results from this?*

Bridget cringed, thinking of the three months for the GCG recommendations and three months of her team trying to implement their recommendations with zero progress.

- *What's your timetable for getting started?*

Bridget paused when she heard a voice heading her way.

"Get this, the new consultant is going to take two years! … Can you believe it? … I agree—the board will never let it drag on that long."

Bridget thought it was her CIO, Andrea, but wanted to be sure. She heard a car door open, and she turned to look.

"Who'd you hear that from? … I think they're probably right. Bridget will be gone by the end of the—uh, I'll call you back."

No! thought Andrea as she returned Bridget's wave with a smile and a wave of her own. Keeping the smile on her face, Andrea started up her car and pulled out of the lot, praying that Bridget hadn't heard her end of the conversation.

THE TRANSFORMATION BEGINS

"Listen up, everyone. No matter what doubts you may still have about this new initiative, it's imperative that we all present a united front, because this is the direction Talon Tech is moving. Any remaining concerns you have, you can address them to me directly." Bridget let her gaze linger a beat longer on Andrea. "Is that understood?" Everyone on the leadership team nodded their assent as they stood huddled backstage in Talon Tech's auditorium.

"Excuse me, Bridget," said Nick, her assistant.

"Yes, Nick."

"Everyone is seated, and all our external locations are online. We're ready to go when you are."

"Thank you, Nick. Let's go," Bridget said as she led her team onto the stage. Stepping up to the podium, Bridget looked out to her audience and smiled. "Good morning, all!" She then looked at each monitor at the back of the auditorium. "Good evening, Singapore; good afternoon, London and Lisbon; good early morning to Los

Angeles and Santa Fe!" Bridget continued until she had acknowledged each of Talon Tech's offices not physically present. "I thank you all for being here." There was a smattering of applause. Bridget swallowed hard, cleared her throat, and threw herself into the speech she and Ray had crafted.

"Talon Tech is incredibly fortunate to be the leader in wearable technology. Wearable technology that improves the lives of our customers." Bridget paused and once again looked at the audience sitting in the auditorium and each team represented on the monitors. "This incredible fortune is not luck. It is the result of the hard work, commitment, and innovative spirit that all of you bring to the table." That garnered a loud round of applause with a few *woots* thrown in.

Buoyed by their enthusiasm, Bridget rallied them on. "Are you ready to take Talon Tech to the next level?"

More applause and a wave of "Yes!" filled the auditorium.

"I'm glad to hear it," said Bridget, laughing, "because Talon Tech is ready to release the full potential of each and every one of us here today. I am so proud of the work we have accomplished together, and I am excited about the unlimited opportunities that lie ahead for all of us. I understand that we have some real challenges ahead and that we …" Bridget turned to face her leadership team sitting behind her and then turned back to the podium … "as your leadership team must do better." That drew some murmurs and head nods from the audience.

"What I promise you today," Bridget continued, "is that everyone on this stage is wholly committed to providing each and every one of you the support, tools, and training needed to be the best you can be and to elevate Talon Tech to the next level."

That prompted another round of applause and a shout of "Finally!"

"To kick off our commitment to releasing our full potential, every one of us will participate in an experience like none other. We will all embark on an adventure across the vast and perilous desert in search of gold," Bridget said with a gleam in her eye. "Next week, Talon Tech's leadership team will be the first to cross the desert—wish us luck! And over the next few weeks, your direct leaders will be coordinating your opportunity to journey across the desert in search of gold."

Someone in the front raised their hand and asked, "What do you mean we are going to cross a desert?"

Bridget smiled and said, "I know this doesn't make sense right now, but I promise it will. Thank you all again for being here today. I know that for some of you it's either quite late or quite early, and I appreciate you making the time to be here with us. Stay tuned for dates and training locations of your 'desert adventure,' and don't forget to stay hydrated!"

Bridget and her team exited the stage to a variety of mumblings, including "What was that all about?" and "I hope she meant it when she said leadership is finally going to support us." Although her audience was left a bit confused, Bridget felt good about the meeting. Ray confirmed her feelings. "That was perfect, Bridget," he said as they left the auditorium together.

The following week went by in a blur for Bridget—coordinating the company-wide communications around the initiative with Harry, as head of HR, and Ray and his team as well as the daily running of Talon Tech. The highlight of the week had come on Friday, when the executive leadership team and their VPs had raced across the desert in search of the Gold of the Desert Kings. It was their first exposure to Ray's "experiential learning," and it had been both highly engaging and tremendously insightful.

The thought of how many of them had epically failed to come out of the desert alive made her laugh. But the shared failures and successes had provided the opportunity to look at how they could have all crossed successfully and how the lessons they derived from the experience were immediately applicable to improving Talon Tech's performance. The experience had also connected them on a deeper level as a team—even Gisela had fully immersed herself in the experience without once grumbling about the lack of access to her phone, and with Gisela on board, so, too, was Jordan. If their commitment in this meeting could transfer to the full initiative, that would be a tremendous step forward.

But now it was Monday morning once again, and the initiative's company-wide communication strategies were at the forefront of the next phase of the rollout. Bridget's bracelet chimed just as Nick poked his head in the door. "Yup, I know," she said with a smile. "Time to head over to the marketing department to meet with Samantha and Ray."

"Are you sure I'm the right person to kick this off, Ray?" asked Samantha. "I market products, not initiatives."

"I am positive you are!" said Bridget as she walked into Samantha's office. "Your skill at presenting a product effectively makes you the right person to present the initiative clearly."

"I don't know, Bridget. Won't it have more impact if people hear it from you?"

"No," interrupted Ray. "Bridget committed the whole of the leadership team to release the full potential of every employee, and every employee needs to see that commitment from everyone on the leadership team."

"I get it," said Samantha nervously.

"Okay, great," said Ray. "Now, you've worked with us on the script, and you and I walked through it a few times last week. You feel comfortable with it, yes?"

"I think so," said Samantha.

"You can do as many takes as you like until you *know* you're comfortable. When you feel you're ready, the AV crew here will turn the camera on. If you don't like the playback, they'll reshoot—no big deal. The script will be running on the teleprompter, but feel free to ad lib as you go."

"Okay," said Samantha. "That makes me feel better."

"Great," said Ray. "Remember, you'll have a chance to review the final version before we post it."

Ray and Bridget moved to the small conference table at the back of Samantha's office to review the final training schedule that all employees would go through over the next five weeks. Before they got too far, Samantha was pulling up a chair. "Well, that was quick and painless," she said.

"I told you," said Ray. "We make it as easy for you as possible. Now, let's finish reviewing the training options and sign-up procedures to make sure we've addressed all your concerns, Samantha."

Samantha turned to Bridget. "I told Ray that I wanted to make sure we gave people enough opportunities to go through the training. Given that it's mandatory, I wanted to make sure that if someone already had scheduled vacation time off or were sick during their scheduled time, they could join another group's training."

"Great," said Bridget, making a check mark in her Transformation Notebook. "That was on my list for Ray as well." It was still strange to be pulling out and writing in a paper notebook, and she had taken a lot of grief from the team about it, but it had helped Bridget find a rhythm through this process, and she was determined to stick with it.

Later that afternoon, emails from members of the leadership team and VPs started popping up in Samantha's inbox with comments about her video that had just been blasted company wide.

Love the desert attire, wrote DeAngela. *Nice touch!*

You've definitely piqued my department's interest, wrote Harry.

My team is asking me if the experience was as great as you made it sound, to which I replied, "Absolutely!" wrote Dishant.

Samantha's nervousness around the campaign was subsiding, and she was beginning to enjoy the process. She couldn't wait to see the responses to the Gold of the Desert King water bottles that would be appearing on everyone's desks over the next couple of weeks … along with a secret code that would grant them access into the oasis to sign up for their own desert crossing.

CROSSING THE VAST AND PERILOUS DESERT

Harry caught up with Bridget in the break room. "You're brave having a big cup of coffee this late in the day, Bridget."

"I know. I tried to talk myself out of it, but it's been a crazy day, and I find coffee comforting. Maybe just cradling it in my hands and enjoying its aroma will be enough," she said. "How are things?"

"It's the last week of the Gold of the Desert King experiences. I don't want to jinx it, but so far we've only had a couple of hiccups that were easily resolved."

Bridget smiled. "Kudos to you and your HR team. I have heard nothing but positive feedback—mostly just from conversations I've been overhearing in the halls and here in the break room. People are buzzing, Harry!"

"They are, and we need to keep building on it," said Harry as he grabbed a juice from the fridge. "I'm sorry I haven't responded to the email you sent to the exec team asking for status updates related to the initiative, but it will be in your inbox first thing tomorrow morning."

"Sounds good. I'm going to go back to my office now and enjoy not drinking my coffee," said Bridget with a grin. "Good luck on the final week of training."

The day of the final training session arrived, and Dishant, who had kicked off the first three sessions, wanted to do the honors of kicking off the final one. He jogged the few feet to the podium. "Good morning, everyone!" he said, beaming.

"Good morning!" roared the room, pleased to see the CFO there with them in person to kick off the session.

"You," said Dishant as his eyes scanned the room, "are about to race across the vast and perilous desert, so I hope you are feeling rested and energized!"

"We are!" came excited shouts.

"You are the final teams to race across the desert! I warn you, it's not as easy as it may appear, but the lessons and insights you take away from this experience will fire you up! And that collective fire is what will empower us to release the full potential of everyone at Talon Tech!" Dishant turned to Ray's team member, Gloria. "Gloria is here to facilitate your experience this morning. Good luck, everyone! And don't forget to have fun."

"Good morning, ladies and gentlemen," began Gloria. "As Dishant just told you, in just a few moments you will be racing across the vast and perilous desert! I'm glad to see everyone has brought their water bottles—you're going to need them, because it's going to get hot out there!"

"I don't care what they dress this up as, we all know that eventually it will turn into the same PowerPoint-type presentation we've sat through a million times," the distribution manager at table four whispered to the person next to her.

"Look around at the people at your table," said Gloria, "because they are who you will be trekking across the desert with. Your lives will depend on each other."

There were murmurs and bits of nervous laughter as people surveyed their tablemates.

"Now, look around at your colleagues sitting at the other tables. You will see there are five teams of five, and you will all be racing against each other to see who can bring back as much gold as possible. I'd like you to look at the map in the center of your table," instructed Gloria. "In the bottom right-hand corner you'll see home base. Put your finger there. That's where we are. We're at home base right now." Everyone did as she said. "While at home base, you have resources available to you."

A young man raised his hand. "Yes?" asked Gloria.

"I'm sorry to interrupt. My name is Steve, and I just started here a couple of weeks ago working on the line, and my supervisor sent me here for training, but this doesn't seem like the training I'm supposed to be in, and like I said, I'm new, and I don't want to get in trouble."

"I assure you," said Gloria with a smile, "that you are in the right place."

The young man sat back down and looked around at his team, who seemed to be almost as uncertain as he was.

"Open the envelope at your table, and you will see what those resources are," Gloria continued.

"We've got money," shouted one of the participants, waving it in the air.

"And a camel!" shouted another, laughing.

"That's right," said Gloria, "You all have money, a camel, and a few other resources to get you started. Now, put your finger at the upper left-hand corner. You see those mountains up there?"

"Yes," murmured several people.

"Well, there's gold in those mountains! You are going to cross the vast and perilous desert, which is laid out on the map in front of you, until you get to the mountains. And when you get to the mountains, you're going to get as much gold as possible and bring it back to home base. How much gold are you going to get?" she asked.

More random murmurs from the group. "No, no, no," chided Gloria. "I can't hear you …"

"As much gold as possible," everyone cheered.

"And what are you going to do with that gold?" Gloria asked, cupping her hand to her ear and leaning forward.

"Bring it back to home base," everyone replied with gusto.

"Great," cheered Gloria. "Now, the first team back to home base with their gold is going to get more money for their gold than the second team, who's going to get more than the third team, etc. I mean, it's supply and demand, right?"

"Right!" was the collective and unprompted response.

"To do this, you are going to have twenty-five days to make this trek to the mountains and return to home base. At points during your trek, there will be sandstorms and times of superheat that will make crossing the desert very challenging. Each day will go so fast, it will seem like three minutes. So, every three minutes will count as a day, and you will be allowed to make one move to cross the desert. Now, look at your map again. You'll see there are contiguous squares. Every day, you are allowed to move from the square you're on to any other adjacent square—but you are not required to move if you don't want to. Everyone with me?" asked Gloria.

There were vigorous head nods and conspiratorial looks among tablemates as they eyed their competition.

"Okay," she continued. "If you look at the map, you will see that the most direct route to the mountains is six squares and through the mysterious Tomb of Kings, which would take you how long?"

"Six days!" shouted the group.

"And how many days do you have?"

"Twenty-five!" shouted the group.

"Then you have to get back to home base, right?"

"Right!"

"So, that's another six days, which means you will have to spend a minimum of twelve days traveling." Gloria reviewed all the resources available to them on their journey and reminded them that the goal was to get back to home base with as much gold as possible within twenty-five days and that every day they spent in the mountain, they added one bar of gold to their treasure. "Remember, the first team back gets more money for their gold than any other team. And the amount you get is printed on a sheet of paper in your envelope."

Teams began whispering among themselves and pointing to the map.

"In just a few minutes, I'll give you some time to get to know your team members, do some planning, and go to the 'bank' at the back of the room to buy whatever supplies you feel you will need, but first there is one last bit of information I want to share with you. At home base, there's an old man who loves to talk to people. He claims to know four things about the desert: superheat, sandstorms, water, and the mountains. He's very lonely, so talking to him about any one topic takes one day, and remember, he has information to share on four topics." Gloria paused to make sure she had everyone's attention. "Okay, your planning time has begun!"

Conversations began around the tables, and in a few minutes Gloria said, "Okay, day one has just begun." The teams moved or didn't every three minutes for the first four days. Then the first sandstorm hit and lasted three days. Those who hadn't purchased tents to protect their food and water and those who now realized they hadn't purchased enough food and water to hold them over the full twenty-five days needed to adjust their plans so they could replenish once the storm had passed.

The sandstorm now gone, the teams were on the move again. There were occasional moans about setbacks and slow progress. Then finally, around day ten, whoops were heard from the first team to reach the mountains. Day twelve brought the first deaths. The members of team three died from lack of water. The vultures began to circle. This created anxiety and increasing disagreements among the remaining teams about how and when they should return to home base.

By day fifteen, the superheat hit and lasted two days, impacting everyone but those who were already in the protective range of mountains. As each team monitored the progress of their competitors, disagreements began to emerge about how many days should be spent collecting gold versus getting back to home base as quickly as possible.

At day twenty-one, team five was the first to return. They had three bars of gold and were jubilant at having survived. Team one reached home base on day twenty-five with five bars of gold and were disappointed they weren't the first to finish. Teams two and four didn't make it back in time. As Gloria called a close to day twenty-five, everyone leaned back in their chairs, laughing and clapping each other on the back.

"Okay, everyone, you've just been through an ordeal," said Gloria with a grin. "Let's take a ten-minute break, and then we'll debrief together."

"That was great!" said the distribution manager as she got up to stretch her legs and grab something cold to drink. "And way better than death by PowerPoint. I'm looking forward to the discussion and debrief."

While the desert experience was in progress, the leadership team had gathered for a meeting. DeAngela was the last to arrive. "Wow, this is quite the spread," she said, glancing around at the outlay of cheese boards, fruit salad, and three types of quiche arranged on the side table. "And is that what I think it is?" she asked, turning to Bridget.

"Yes, it is," said Bridget, smiling. "My famous chocolate torte with fresh raspberries."

"I'm thinking what you're thinking, DeAngela," said Tyler with a laugh. "There's some big ask coming."

"Yup, that's exactly what I'm thinking," said DeAngela. She took a seat at the table. "We know what your chocolate torte means, Bridget, so just lay it on us. What are you buttering us up for?"

"Actually, this time my baking talents have been employed to thank you all for a job well done. Truly," she said looking at each member of her team. "I know it was a lot to have the entire company go through the Gold of the Desert Kings in just six weeks, and I appreciate all your efforts. A special thank-you to Harry and Samantha, who collaborated to make the necessary human resources and marketing resources available."

"Does that mean Sam and I get the first piece of cake?" Harry asked, eyes wide in anticipation as he headed toward the food.

Everyone eagerly filled their plates and then gave Ray their full attention.

"I, too, applaud all your efforts these past two months," said Ray. "The great news is, we're beginning to see some initial positive results for all those efforts, as indicated in all your department status updates.

Those department status updates will be due to Bridget at the end of each month—it's all part of the accountability loop that will be implemented throughout the organization.

"Next week, we begin rolling out the people-first training, right on schedule. This is all good work, but we're just getting started. Let's walk through the trajectory of all the components of the initiative over the next two years, after which we will zero in on everyone's role in the next three months to capitalize on all the positive energy generated by the Gold of the Desert Kings experience."

The group spent the next ninety minutes walking through Ray's detailed Gantt chart of their trajectory over the next two years. They covered how and when each component of leadership, communication, alignment, training, reinforcement, and metrics would be implemented.

"Thanks, everyone, for your input today. Because of everyone's commitment to this initiative, Bridget has early positive indications that will demonstrate to the board that Talon Tech is on the right path. Now, before we go," Ray said, "I want to make sure everyone has scheduled their monthly videos over the next ten months. Remember, every month, we need one of you to film a seven-minute video that will go out company wide to update everyone on the status of the initiative."

"Ray, we're talking about the initiative in every single meeting, we're sending out departmental updates to teams every week, and it's highlighted in Talon Tech's monthly newsletter. Is it really necessary to have us also spend time doing videos when we could be getting more important things done?" interjected Andrea.

"Yes, Andrea, it is. As we've discussed, the leadership team, which most definitely includes you as CIO, serves as the lead, guide, and cheerleader for this initiative. Newsletters simply can't garner the level of interest and enthusiasm that Samantha's and Dishant's videos did. We want you to demonstrate your commitment to the initiative and share some stories. If you're comfortable sharing from your own perspective, great. If you want us to write a script for you, we will do that. Whatever is best to set you up for success, we'll do, but it does need to be done. Please make sure that before you leave today, you schedule the month in which your video will be filmed."

"Walk with me," DeAngela said to Andrea as they left the meeting. "What is up with you? Why do you keep poking the bear? Some good things are happening because of this initiative. You must see that."

"What I see," said Andrea, "is a CEO of *the* leading tech company who is pivoting her priorities away from technology. We are not a people company; we are a technology company, and I'm going to do what I can to make sure we keep Talon Tech's focus where it should be—on its technology!"

"Andrea," DeAngela asked as her colleague turned and began to walk away, "what does that even mean?" But before she could finish her sentence, Andrea had already turned the corner and was out of sight.

Meanwhile, back at the desert experience, Gloria nearly needed to shout to be heard over the buzz of conversation in the room. "I'm going to ask everyone to return to their seats for the debrief, please." She was always glad to see colleagues from all different departments and levels of the company connecting for the first time. Everyone was always so reserved and uncertain at first, but by the end of their treks across the desert, they had a newfound interest in and respect for each other.

"So, how many of you talked to the old man?" Gloria asked the group.

A team member from table five was the only one to raise a hand. "Hi again, Steve," Gloria said with a smile. "Why, and what did your team ask the old man?"

"Well, we wanted to make sure we didn't lose all our supplies in one of the sandstorms, so we asked him about that. It helped us plan our supplies better, and we bought a tent to keep them safe as a result. That saved us a few days of traveling to replenish."

"Great. Now, why didn't any other teams talk to the old man?"

"We only had twenty-five days. We couldn't afford to spend four of those days talking to a lonely old man," were the common replies.

"Okay," said Gloria. "It sounds like in your rush to get to where you were going and get back, you didn't feel the need to gather all the available information about how to get there and back safely and quickly. Is that right?"

"Yeah, I guess so," was one response.

"When you put it like that, we don't sound very smart," said another, laughing.

Together, Gloria walked them through how gathering information up front on how best to reach their collective goal of *as much gold as possible*, effectively utilizing that information, and mapping out a plan based on that data would have garnered each team not three bars like team five, or even five bars like team one, but ten bars for every team.

"What were some of the team obstacles you faced along the way?"

"Well, we didn't communicate well, because none of us really understood what we were up against," offered a member of team three. "And that didn't work out so well for us—we're all still out there having our bones picked clean by the vultures!"

That got a laugh from the whole room. "That is a significantly bad consequence," Gloria agreed. "What other team obstacles did you face?"

"Well, some of us," offered a young woman, sending a glance to the distribution manager on her team, "just wouldn't listen to anyone else's ideas."

The distribution manager reddened a bit. "You're right, Kelly. I really didn't, and because of that our team is still wandering around out there."

As the debrief continued, Gloria began to shift the conversation to how their desert experience and learnings from it applied directly to their jobs in the company. "Thank you all for your active participation today and your honesty on why no one was as successful as they could have been. At Talon Tech, our goal is to get ten bars of gold every time. What do ten bars of gold look like for Talon Tech?"

As a group, they began to make a list:

- Great customer service

- Great products

- Using all the resources that we have at our disposal

- Willingness to share what we know

- Determining what are the things that we need to win

- Great sales revenues *and* great employee engagement

They continued the conversation, equating what their survival needs from the desert looked like for Talon Tech. Food was equated to the quality of their product, and water was equated with the service they provided to their customers. Everyone agreed that those necessities were useless unless they utilized them as a team and not as individuals. They dug into the obstacles that were getting in the way of Talon Tech achieving ten bars of gold in all these areas and how the lessons from their desert experience could be immediately and directly applied to help make that a reality.

"Great work, everyone," said Gloria, bringing the morning session to a close. "We are beginning a journey now over the next two years to continually get Talon Tech ten bars of gold. And you are vital to that journey. Every one of you, whether you're an executive, a line worker, or a supervisor, offers tremendous value, because you are like the old men in this organization. And we need to value what you have to say, and to do that, we will better equip your leaders so that you can share that information, feel supported, and commit to your role in the journey.

"Now, information gained from the old man is not the whole journey," she continued. "People can talk to the old man and still die in the desert if they don't apply his information effectively, buy the right amount of food or water, or take the wrong path. The old man is not a silver bullet, but his knowledge is an important component. Let's break for lunch, and when we return, we'll apply some practical training techniques to the obstacles you've all just identified."

It was nearly five when Bridget received the text that the final Desert Kings training was a success and that everyone left energized and eager to achieve ten bars of gold moving forward. *The wins are beginning to add up*, she thought as she headed out to meet Natasha and Marty.

Bridget arrived at the Brown Pelican half an hour before her friends. She needed a few minutes to catch up on her Transformation Notebook before they arrived:

Applications applied from Gold of the Desert Kings:
- *Know and get agreement on what "ten bars of gold" looks like for all major objectives.*

- *Take time to gather all available information and to plan to achieve all that's possible.*

- *Use all team members' insight and skill.*

- *Deal with the unknown head on: don't avoid it.*

As CEO, remember this:
- *The power of investing in everyone:*
    □ *Common language*

    □ *Common understanding*

    □ *Respect for every individual regardless of rank*

- *The positive impact of our senior leaders setting the pace by example*

- *Not to confuse early wins with ultimate success—stay the course!*

- *The importance of giving the whole team the full picture of our two-year plan*

"Hi!" Natasha's voice jerked Bridget from her thoughts. "Didn't mean to startle you, Bridget," Natasha said as she took the seat across from Bridget, hooking the handle of her pocketbook on the back of the chair.

"So, are you ready for the board meeting?" asked Marty, slipping into the seat next to Natasha.

"Where did you come from?" asked Natasha with surprise.

"I was right behind you for almost a block. You nearly hit me with the door when I walked in behind you!"

"Yeah, right. You probably just slunk over from the bar."

The three of them laughed as Bridget put away her notebook and handed them the menus the waiter had left on the table when Bridget first arrived.

"Well, in answer to your question, I'm as ready as I'm going to be. Thank you, both, for grabbing a bite to eat with me and steadying my nerves before the board meeting begins," said Bridget.

"You got this," said Marty. "I mean, you've had our incredible wisdom to draw on. How could you not be?" he said with a wink.

"Right," said Bridget, laughing. "It's your shared wisdom that's going to make this all work."

Over sandwiches and a shared basket of fries, Bridget brought them both up to date on how things were going with Ray and some of the challenges she had encountered with the leadership team.

"That's my cue," she said when one of her beads chimed. "Five forty-five—the moment of truth has arrived." Bridget stood and pulled her coat from the back of her chair. "If all goes according to plan, I'll be walking back over here shortly after seven for a celebratory drink. Let me know if you decide to head out before I get back."

"We'll be here," said Marty.

"Yeah, we have plenty to catch up on and lots of desserts to sample!" said Natasha. "Now, go."

"Right on time," said Natasha as Bridget sat back down next to her. She looked at her watch. "Seven twenty—that's either really good news or …"

"She's smiling," said Marty encouragingly. "Good news, right?"

Bridget let out a long, slow breath, "Yeah," she said, smiling. "Good news. I'm still CEO of Talon Tech for the foreseeable future."

Natasha caught their server's eye, and they ordered a round of drinks.

"To Bridget and Talon Tech," said Marty, raising his glass. Natasha and Bridget raised theirs, and they all took a sip of their martinis. "Now, spill," he said. "We want to hear every detail."

Before she could answer, Bridget's phone dinged. "Don't you look at that," said Natasha. "Enjoy your moment of celebration."

"It could be Rob. I'm just going to check really quick. If it's not him, my phone goes away."

She looked back up at her friends. "You were right—I should have just enjoyed the moment, because it's already gone."

"What are you talking about?"

"This is from my COO." She held up her phone so they could read DeAngela's text.

We have a problem. A big one. I've just been informed that the chips that activate car heaters have a glitch and complaints are piling up. Seems this has been a problem for a while, but now that the cold weather has set in, it's morphed into a huge one. Meet you in your office first thing tomorrow?

We'll meet immediately following the company-wide meeting, Bridget texted back.

A POTENTIAL
DERAILING

Bridget and Ray exited the coffee shop, navigating the steady flow of people heading in for their morning cup of joe. Eyes glued to their phones, they would shoot Bridget a look of annoyance every time they bumped into her. "Really?" she wanted to say, but she had more important things to focus her energies on.

"Well," she said as she took off her coat and draped it on the back of her chair, "at least today's unexpected warm weather won't require anyone to turn their car heaters on!"

Ray took the seat across from her at one of the small tables on the sidewalk in front of the shop. "I like your optimism."

"It wasn't optimism that I was channeling," she said, removing the lid from her cup and letting the steam and its aroma waft up in front of her face.

"Yeah, I got that," said Ray with a smile, "but there really is a silver lining here."

"You can't be serious," Bridget said, holding up her phone. "You've already seen DeAngela's text, but you haven't seen all of Andrea's angry texts. I haven't dared to listen to her voicemails. I just let her know that we will meet to address the issue after the company-wide meeting. Which we need to write a whole new speech for. Thank you, Ray, for meeting me so early to get this done in time," Bridget said, setting her tablet and keyboard on the table.

Ray put his cup down. "What do you mean, a new speech?"

"Ray, I have a serious technical problem for which I haven't identified the source, and customer service complaints have seemingly skyrocketed overnight."

"And?" Ray asked.

"And? And I don't see how I can go out in front of the entire company and talk about our initial improvements and how we're going to head into the next round of company training when all this is going on."

"I get that this feels like a huge setback, and I'm not minimizing the seriousness of it or the headaches this will cause, but as you agreed, you must stay the course. In this case, it provides us an opportunity to focus the application of the training to this immediate issue, which is a good thing, because then they won't be learning new behaviors in the abstract—they'll be learning them based on a true scenario."

"You can do that?" asked Bridget.

"Yes, we'll make every case study, every scenario, every situation they are wrestling with in the class relevant to the chip issue. They'll review the decision that led to this issue and some of the real customer complaints that resulted from that decision. Then they'll assess it against the decision-making model that we want them to implement for all decisions going forward."

"Even still, Andrea's going to keep pushing back about no time for training."

"Yup, she will, and others may too," said Ray. "All the more reason for you to reaffirm to your leadership team and the company your commitment to this initiative. To pull back now would sink any chance of success. You're barely three months in, and you're ready to throw in the towel—"

"I'm not throwing in the towel," Bridget protested. "I'm pressing pause."

"No matter what you call it, Bridget, any later pledge you make to the commitment to harnessing the power of your people will be meaningless. You must stay the course, and everyone on your leadership team must be required to stay the course."

"I can see Andrea using this as a reason to dig her heels in even more about our apparent lack of technology focus, and with my head of sales and head of manufacturing still only just beginning to increase their commitment, she may be able to convince them to dig their heels in, too."

"If that happens, you'll have some tough decisions to make, but we're not there yet." Ray went on to outline their approach going into the meeting with the heads of operations, IT, and manufacturing once the company-wide meeting concluded. "For now," Ray said, "you have a rousing speech to give in ninety minutes. Let's focus on that."

"Good morning, everyone," said Bridget. "I'm incredibly pleased with the feedback from what I think you will all agree was a really cool experience. You told us we needed to do better, and the Gold of the Desert Kings experience showed all of us that Talon Tech can achieve ten bars of gold in every area of the business every time if we learn to behave differently. Because of our collective efforts applying these principles, we're already seeing an uptick in the metrics related to people's engagement, which then improved our customer service metrics. The board is pleased with these early signs that we are on the right track with our new initiative."

"Now, to continue to improve our metrics, we will have to learn how to behave differently on the job. For that to happen, we all need to learn what those new behaviors are, and that learning will come in the training that your leaders will be coordinating for you over the next several weeks. Your leaders will be taking that same training with you, but they will also be taking additional training so that they will be equipped to help you apply the new behaviors and skills on the job. When we all apply those new behaviors and skills, we will consistently acquire our ten bars of gold."

Bridget looked at the screen on her podium. "Dishant has just let me know that your questions are coming in. That's great!"

Dishant joined Bridget on the podium. "Good morning, everyone. For those who don't know me, I'm Dishant Patel, Talon Tech's chief financial officer." He tapped a bead on his bracelet, and the screen behind the podium lit up. "We'll display your questions one at a time, and then Bridget and I will answer them."

"And," Bridget added, "any questions that we don't get to today, or new ones that you think of after the meeting, please know that you can ask your supervisor, their leader, or anyone on the executive leadership team—including me—and we will respond as quickly as possible."

"First question," said Dishant. "'Why new behaviors and skills?' That's a great question. Think about the fact that we're going to have to move mountains to get ten bars of gold every time. To do that, we can't be afraid of the unknowns; we must gather info from all the old men—all of you—to understand each situation as well as possible and to then plan and support each other accordingly. The first thing that we, as your leadership team, are going to do is help you at home base. We're going to load you up with food and water. That food and water is the training that's coming."

"Then," added Bridget, "we're going to load you and your leaders with the tools you need to develop and continue to improve the new skills and behaviors you've learned."

Bridget and Dishant continued to answer questions for the next thirty minutes, letting everyone know that they had hired an expert to guide them through this transformation, that the improvements at first would be incremental—just as they had begun to see in people engagement and customer service—and that this would require the whole company's commitment to a two-year process to realize its full impact. "And yes," Dishant concluded, "I have approved the budget to support all the tools, resources, and training that we have promised."

As they exited the auditorium, Dishant wished Bridget good luck with what they both knew was going to be a tense meeting about the chip issue.

"What I want to know is, how come we didn't hear about the defective chips before it blew up on us?" Andrea looked at DeAngela and Jordan accusingly.

"Are you serious?" asked Jordan. "You're the one who insisted six months ago that we switch to that manufacturer for all the car-related chips, and manufacturing followed your orders."

"And that means I'm responsible for monitoring it? I don't think so." Andrea turned to DeAngela. "Why did none of your customer service people tell us this was a problem?"

"Based on the initial information I have," explained DeAngela, "it appears the issue was infrequent, so when they received the complaint, they took care of the problem and replaced the chip."

"How do they not know to move that type of issue up the chain?" asked Andrea.

"Well," said DeAngela, "as you know, Talon Tech is not a people company—we're a tech company—so, shouldn't you be on top of any technology problems?"

"Okay," said Bridget. "This conversation is not solving the problem. Let's first find where the breakdown happened, so together we can solve it. Ray, I'll let you take it from here."

"Let me guess," said Andrea. "More desert crossings?"

"No," laughed Ray, "No more desert crossings, but definitely more training."

"What we need to do ASAP is put a task force on it so they can do the analysis to figure out what's going on," demanded Andrea.

"That's how you've always managed problems?" asked Ray.

"Yes," said Andrea.

"How's that working for you?" Ray asked. "Right," Ray said when Andrea did not respond. He looked around at the team. "What we're going to do is find out from the frontline people where the problems are and how they think they can be solved. Then we're going to equip the relevant leaders to go and deal with that. Additionally, my team and I are going to adapt the next round of training to working through this real problem, which will put everyone on the same page moving forward."

"Thanks, Ray," said Bridget and then turned to the group. "This will be the first item on the agenda at our morning leadership meeting tomorrow."

As she left the meeting, Andrea's phone buzzed. She quickly declined the call and shot a quick text to the caller, letting him know she'd call him back in ten minutes. Now in her car on the way to her next meeting, she returned the call.

"What is going on over there, Andrea?"

"I know things aren't going exactly as we had planned, Sully, but—"

"Listen, I need to jump soon, and if I'm not going to be jumping to Talon Tech, I need to focus my efforts elsewhere. You said Bridget would be on her way out by now, but I just heard that she announced the board supports the new initiative."

"I know, I know," said Andrea. "A glitch—but that's all it is. I'm telling you, the facade of this people-first initiative is going to crack sooner than later. You'll understand once I tell you about the meeting I just left."

Andrea then shared the situation about the chip problem. "And the consultant's solution is to talk to everyone about the problem and put everyone through more training rather than focusing on getting the right chip ASAP. I'm telling you, Sully, it can't last, and when the board finally sees that, Talon Tech is going to need a truly technology-focused leader like you to take the helm."

"I hope you're right, Andrea, but I've begun a preliminary search of my other options. The clock is ticking over here."

Bridget was glad to head out a few minutes early that afternoon and take a walk in the park to clear her thoughts before picking up the kids. Now waiting in the school parking lot, she took the opportunity to make some clarifying notes in her Transformation Notebook:

- *Trust the process—changing behaviors requires consistency and time.*

- *Support the decision-making process.*

- *Training is best when tailored to real-time issues.*

"How was school today, my loves?" Bridget asked as Craig and Maddie tossed their backpacks onto the floor of the car and hopped into the back seat.

"It was good, Mommy," said Maddie before launching into a monologue of every conversation she had had with her teachers, friends, and afterschool staff that day. Bridget loved Maddie's big personality, but sometimes it overwhelmed her brother. Bridget caught a glimpse of Craig in the rearview mirror. *Yup*, she thought as she watched him tap away on his tablet, *I've already lost him to his game*.

"That all sounds wonderful, Maddie. Hey, sport," Bridget said, trying to catch Craig's eye in the mirror. "Craig?"

"Yeah," he said, finally looking up from the screen.

"Let's put the tablet away, and you tell Maddie and me about your day, please." That garnered her an eye roll, but she was grateful that he still acquiesced easily to most of her requests. By the time they pulled into the driveway, the three of them were engaged in a lively guessing game about the surprise Rob said he was cooking for dinner that night.

As Bridget shrugged off her coat and the kids began yelling guesses as they ran for the kitchen, her watch flashed, and she saw she had an email from Ray.

Here's the outline I promised for the leadership team meeting in the a.m. Have a great night.

Knowing she had about fifteen minutes before Rob would send the kids to tell her dinner was ready, she headed to her office to review the agenda and make notes for the morning's meeting.

The next day came quickly. "Good morning, everyone," said Bridget once all were seated. "We have a lot to cover in the next ninety minutes, so I want to jump right in. DeAngela, can you please give the team an overview of the chip issue that was discovered yesterday, and then Ray will take it from there."

DeAngela explained the issue and how it was discovered, the time frame, and manufacturing's determination that the problem chips had come from a new supplier and accounted for only 20 percent of the beads with the car heater function.

"Thanks, DeAngela," said Ray. "Okay, everyone, we clearly need to solve the problem, and we're going to talk about that in just a minute, but first I need you to decide, as a team, the urgency of the problem."

Andrea leaned forward and opened her mouth to say something, but Ray continued on, and she sat back with a huff.

"Option number one, we put on a full-court press and get everyone through the training in the next four to five weeks to get it behind us. Or, option number two, we take it in stride and resolve it over the next three months. Thoughts?"

Andrea was the first to jump in. "Immediate resolution, without question." She looked around as if to challenge anyone to disagree.

"Well," said Dishant, "I ran some numbers, and it's only affecting one percent of our customer base and a fraction of our total revenue. So, is it really a five-alarm fire worth setting aside other priorities for?"

"But that fraction of revenue, Dishant, doesn't account for the losses that will occur once our quality image is tarnished, and quality is the top Talon Tech feature my sales team relies on to close a lot of deals," said Gisela.

"I hadn't thought of it from that perspective," said Dishant.

"It sounds like we agree it's critical," said Bridget, "but even with the potential for our quality image to take a hit, that hit will be a small percentage of our customer base—and yes, Gisela, I agree that quality is our strength, and we certainly don't want to weaken it. That said, I don't think it's five-alarm critical. I'd give it a yellow urgency as opposed to a red."

"Everyone agree with that?" Ray asked the group.

"I agree, but I don't think we can wait three months, and I get that we don't want to wreak havoc in other areas by trying to get everyone through the next round of training in a matter of weeks," said Gisela, "nor does it sound like we need to."

"How about this," said Ray. "What if we break down how many people are actually involved in the solution and focus on getting that group through the training in the next two to three weeks? Then we can get everyone else through it over the next three months?"

"Great idea," said Bridget.

"Okay," said Ray. "As we identify those people and create the subgroups they belong in, it will be imperative that we also identify the leader of each of those subgroups, because without establishing the cornerstone of leadership, the groups will be far less effective and efficient, leading to a whole lot of frustration for everyone involved."

"That should be easy," said Tyler. "Each of our departments has its own leadership ladder."

"That's true," said Ray. "Within your own functional team you have an established leadership ladder, but this type of issue requires multiple departments on multiple levels to resolve it. It requires cross-functional teams."

"Tyler doesn't like legal to mingle with too many of us outside of his domain," said DeAngela, laughing.

"That's not true," Tyler protested. "It's just that legalities can get murky pretty quickly if everyone isn't knowledgeable about all the potential legal ramifications."

"Well, you'd never survive in operations," said DeAngela, "because to make sure we get our stuff done, we need to work with everyone."

"Nothing changes within the leadership ladder of your func-tional teams," Ray assured them, "but for cross-functional teams to be as effective as possible, you must first gather input from and empower those who are, as DeAngela said, 'getting stuff done,' to make decisions."

Ray moved to the whiteboard wall at the front of the room, uncapped the black marker, and wrote the following:

Cornerstone 1: Leadership

"Okay, we all agree leadership is an essential cornerstone for everything we do, right?" Ray asked the group.

"Right," everyone agreed.

"And we all agree," continued Ray, "that each subgroup will have a designated leader. The leader must be the person accountable for the outcome. For example, the head of sales may be part of a cross-functional team addressing a supply chain issue, but they are not accountable for fixing a supply chain problem, so they can't lead the team. The person in charge of the supply chain, even if lower in rank than the head of sales, would be responsible for the outcome and therefore be the leader. The leader serves as the decision maker, and everyone in their group reports to them on matters related to that subgroup, regardless of their rank. Still with me?"

"Yes … I think we need to see the makeup of the subgroups," said Dishant, "and then we can best determine who should be the leader, correct?"

"Yes," said Ray, "we'll do that, but first we need to determine our goal." Ray exchanged the black marker for a green one and wrote the following:

Cornerstone 2: Unanimous Focus on a Common Goal

"Can we also agree that to achieve anything, everyone involved must first understand what goal we are all striving to achieve?"

Everyone agreed. "Great, so what is the common goal we are trying to achieve here?"

"Our goal is to figure out the root cause of the chip issue and tackle that," said Bridget.

Everyone nodded in agreement. "Okay," said Ray, "what are the subgroups we think we are going to need to solve this problem?"

"Quality," said Gisela. "How did we not know sooner that the chips were defective? We need to find the breakdown."

"I think that would require input from my manufacturing team along with operations and customer service," said Jordan.

Ray nodded. "It looks like our first subgroup includes representatives from manufacturing, operations, and customer service," said Ray, writing the list on the board.

"Customer complaints and refunds need to be addressed," said Samantha, "before it blows up any further."

"And who needs to be in that subgroup?"

"Customer service, obviously, but I also think marketing, sales … and yes, even legal," said Tyler. "What?" he asked in response to the raised eyebrows around the table. "I'm beginning to see the logic of talking with the 'old men' from the related departments before we determine the best way to go after our ten bars of gold."

The group continued to determine the subgroups needed to accomplish their common goal of identifying the root cause of the chip issue and solving it, all the way from procurement through to customer satisfaction. When they finished, five subgroups as well as the individual members and an identified leader of each of the subgroups were written on the whiteboard.

"Great work, everyone. Now we have our subgroups and," he said, uncapping the light blue marker, "we've fulfilled our next cornerstone."

Cornerstone 3: Clearly Defined Roles for Subgroups

"So, how many of these cornerstones are there, Ray?" asked Harry. "I'm already thinking of how we can incorporate them into our HR processes."

Ray's eyes lit up. "Fantastic, Harry! Alignment of all aspects of our people-first initiative must align with Talon Tech's HR policies and procedures. There are seven cornerstones, but for today we'll only talk about the first four. The training you'll be taking in the next two to three weeks will cover all seven. I'm going to let you discover the last three cornerstones alongside your direct reports at the training."

Ray began writing on the whiteboard once again—this time in yellow:

Cornerstone 4: Shared Resources

"What resources do each subgroup need?" prompted Ray. "The resources we are talking about fall into two categories: hard, like people and money, and soft, like ideas and enthusiasm.

"Are there resources in one department that we need to put on the team to solve the problem in another area?

"In the soft category of resources, as you go back to your department to inform the people we've identified to be in a subgroup, please explicitly stress that their input, ideas, observations, and suggestions are not just wanted but are essential. In the training, we'll show how they can best share their thinking, and we'll train the leader on how to encourage and then process that input, leading to action steps.

"In terms of hard resources, we've already agreed who should be on which team, and we will need to wait on recommendations to see what other resources will be required or will need to be shared between or from other functions.

"Again, great work, everyone," said Ray. "Now, we've identified our subgroups, their leaders, and the necessary shared resources. Let's get senior leadership and the other members of the subgroups through the training about how to optimize their performance as a team as quickly as possible. Can everyone commit to that?"

There were yeses all around. There was also a mix of excitement and a bit of nervousness about how this would all play out in the training and if that training would truly translate to the real work of Talon Tech. Specifically, could it address the urgency of the chip problem?

THE SEVEN CORNERSTONES

elcome to Tongo's Tower," said DeAngela and Gisela as they handed out three-foot-long clear plastic tubes filled with all kinds of stuff to each team seated in the conference room.

"What is this for?" everyone asked.

"No idea," DeAngela and Gisela responded. "We'll be finding out what we're doing with these tubes right along with you!"

"Good morning, everyone!"

"Good morning, Bridget!"

"I'm so glad you are all as excited as I am to experience our next training adventure together, and by the looks on your faces, I would say you are also just as confused as I am about what we will be doing with Tongo and the tubes on everyone's table," said Bridget, laughing. "One thing I'm certain of is the applicable lessons we will take away from our experience today, an experience that Gloria and Jason will lead us through. So, are we ready to have some fun?"

Gloria approached the podium amid shouts of "Yes!" and fist pumps in the air as Bridget took a seat with her team. "Good morning, everyone!" said Gloria. "I'm excited for all the experiences you will be participating in today, and to kick it off, you'll be building a tower for Tongo!"

"In today's world," began Jason as he walked in and around the tables, "people have primarily cats and dogs for pets, but there has been an increase in monkeys as pets. As a result of that increase, we believe there's an opportunity to provide a product that allows people to build climbing towers for their pet monkeys. I'm going to ask you all to free Tongo from the tube on your table."

"I'm free! I'm free!" sang one of the participants, waving the stuffed monkey over his head.

"Now that Tongo is free," said Jason, "he needs something to keep him out of trouble. Your task is to build the tallest tower possible for Tongo using the materials in your tubes. When Gloria says go, you will have fifteen minutes to build your tallest tower. Is everyone ready?"

"Yes," everyone cheered.

"Go!" said Gloria.

For the next fifteen minutes, the six teams of executive leaders and members of the subgroups assigned to the chip issue frantically mixed and matched Popsicle sticks, rubber bands, pipe cleaners, paper clips, and the other random items in an attempt to build their towers. Added to the mix were bursts of laughter, collaborative conversations, and a few heated discussions.

"And … stop!" called Gloria.

Everyone plopped back into their chairs. "Well, that felt chaotic," said one of the AVPs from manufacturing.

"Yeah, and frustrating," said Tyler.

"Feeling a bit chaotic and frustrating is a common response," said Gloria. "Now, Jason is going to measure everyone's tower to see how much success you were able to eke out of that chaos and frustration."

"Drum roll, please," said Jason, and everyone immediately began tapping on the tables with increasing speed. "The tallest tower, standing at two feet, three inches was built by … team two!"

The members of team two were on their feet cheering in celebration.

"Congratulations," said Gloria. "Now, do you want to know how tall you *could* have built your towers?"

"Only if it's not taller than two feet, three inches," shouted Sandy, the customer call center lead for the northeast division on team two. That brought a ripple of laughter across the room.

"I'm afraid it's a bit taller than that," said Gloria as she held up a photo of a seven-foot Tongo tower.

There were moans and a few mumbles of "That's not possible."

"It *is* possible," said Jason. "So, what do you think caused all of you to only get between one and four bars of gold instead of all ten bars of gold?"

"We had no plan," said Andrea.

"We didn't understand how to use the materials we were given," said Samantha.

"And everyone had their own ideas of how to build the tower and talked over each other to get their ideas heard," said the line tech of the technology division.

"So, left to your own devices, and with your current skill sets, you didn't perform well as effective teams," Jason summed up. "Let us tell you why."

Jason and Gloria introduced the concept of the Seven Cornerstones of Teamwork. They walked the group through the first four cornerstones—leadership, unanimous focus on a common goal, clearly defined roles for subgroups, and shared resources—in much the same way that Ray had walked the executive leadership team through them the week before.

"Okay," said Gloria. "Now let's talk about the fifth principle of teamwork. Has anyone ever had anyone explain an idea or process to you, after which you walked away scratching your head and wondering, *What did they just say?*" Everyone shot up a hand.

"The most frustrating part," said Harry, "is that the person who just did the explaining walks away believing you understand what they just said. We see this all the time in HR when people come in thinking a policy means one thing when the intention of the policy is quite different."

"You're right, Harry," said Gloria. "Effective message delivery and effective message receipt are often confused. If everyone on the team cannot clearly and consistently understand the message *and* clearly and consistently communicate the message, then it's not effective.

"Frequency is the other key component. If the core message being communicated is not resurfaced with enough frequency, it can easily get lost in the overwhelming amount of information we receive every day."

Jason picked up the purple marker and added the following to the list:

Cornerstone 5: Effective and Frequent Communication

"Now, these five cornerstones should be everything we need to lead a team effectively, right?" Jason asked the group.

"Well," said Sandy, "yes and no."

"Tell us what you mean, Sandy," said Jason.

"Those cornerstones definitely establish the structure, but we humans—at least the ones at my call center—if left to our own devices can be a pretty inconsistent bunch, and so we need something to keep us all motivated and applying consistent effort no matter where we are in the day or the process."

"Excellent!" said Jason. He wrote the following on the wall in dark blue:

Cornerstone 6: Consistent, United, and Enthusiastic Effort

"It's important," he continued, "that every member of the team bring to the team's committed outcome a consistent and enthusiastic mindset. This not only keeps the focus on performance excellence but also means that one team member's poor attitude won't negatively influence everyone else."

"Now for our seventh and final cornerstone," began Gloria. "If you think back on your experience searching for the Gold of the Desert Kings and building Tongo's Tower today, is there anything else that comes to mind as a stumbling block to great teamwork?"

Everyone was quiet for a minute.

"When one person dominates and puts their focus on their own personal goals or perspective rather than keeping their focus and efforts on the team's goals. Doing so can create tension for the whole team," said DeAngela, glancing across the room at Andrea. Andrea quickly looked away.

"Yes!" said Gloria. "While a healthy dose of ego is necessary, there are times when we let it override the interests of the whole. It's also just as bad when someone with something valuable to contribute just stays silent. To adjust for this, we must incorporate our final cornerstone."

Jason wrote the following in red:

Cornerstone 7: Periodic and Temporary Suppression of the Ego

"It's important to reiterate the *periodic* and *temporary* aspect of this cornerstone. It is not about permanently suppressing your ego; it is knowing when to suppress it and when not to suppress it," explained Jason before turning to Gloria.

"Each of these cornerstones is critical to a team's success and should set the standard for every team's behavior," said Gloria. "Everyone in this room is aware of the chip problem that we need to resolve, and we're going to provide you the opportunity to apply the Seven Cornerstones of Teamwork to help you solve it as efficiently as possible. But before we do that, we're going to give you all a well-deserved lunch break."

Bridget ducked out of the training session quickly and headed across the courtyard toward her office. She needed to go over her schedule with Nick. She had budget meetings with ops and manufacturing on Wednesday and wanted to make sure he had blocked out time tomorrow so she could finish going over the projections that sales and manufacturing had sent over last week. Plus, she needed to move up the meeting she and Tyler were having with the contractor for the London office to address the legal challenges they were facing with the city's building control office.

Meet me in the small conference room, she texted to Nick as she entered the building. She knew that if she went to her office, she would not be able to focus on the things she needed to get done before the lunch break was over.

"Thank you, Nick," Bridget said with a smile as she eyed the roast-turkey-and-avocado sandwich sitting on the table for her. She was famished and wasted no time taking her first bite and chasing it down with a swig of the ice-cold lemonade Nick had just set down for her. "You are a lifesaver. This sandwich is delicious."

"I'm glad you like it," said Nick. He tapped a bead on his wrist, and the screen at the front of the room lit up. Bridget's eyes went wide.

"I know," said Nick, "but I promise it's not quite as impossible as it seems. Several of the items are short blocks of ten or fifteen minutes for department head updates."

"Okay," said Bridget and rattled off the list of schedule changes she needed to make, including blocks of time to get stuff done.

"You got it," said Nick, getting up and pushing in his chair. "I'll ding you when everything's been updated in your calendar," he said as he left the conference room and headed back to his desk.

Bridget looked at her watch. She had almost twenty minutes until the training resumed, minus the four-minute walk back. She took the last bite of her sandwich, wiped her mouth with her napkin, and pushed the plate aside. "Email time," she said softly as she pushed the small button on the table that illuminated the built-in keyboard and tapped a bead on her bracelet to pull her email up onto the big screen.

She shot off a few quick emails but decided she didn't have time to respond to DeAngela's latest email:

Just an FYI, on the safety front we've had a small uptick in near misses in the distribution area in the last thirty days. Monitoring it and will keep you updated.

"And we're back!" said Gloria. "We've got a lot more to do, so let's jump into it. Are you ready to see why these seven team standards are called cornerstones?"

"Yes!" was the group reply.

"Great," said Gloria as she handed each individual a bag filled with seven small glass stones. The color of each one represented one of the seven team principles. Included with their stones was a code to download an app that could be used in place of their physical stones if they preferred.

As a group they then reviewed the Seven Cornerstones of Teamwork:

1. Leadership—black

2. Unanimous Focus on a Common Goal—green

3. Clearly Defined Roles for Subgroups—light blue

4. Shared Resources—yellow

5. Effective and Frequent Communication—purple

6. Consistent, United, and Enthusiastic Effort—dark blue

7. Periodic and Temporary Suppression of the Ego—red

"All of us comprise the team charged with resolving the chip issue, and we've identified DeAngela as the overall Black Stone Leader. However, to tackle the issue as efficiently as possible, we've set up five subgroups. Each subgroup is a team of its own with its own Black Stone Leader assigned. Each subgroup's Black Stone Leader will bring your work back to the larger team. The subgroups are," Gloria continued, "procurement, quality, manufacturing, technology, and customer service.

"Each group has been provided the clearly defined roles for their subgroup, and you have in front of you the customer complaints that led us to the discovery of the faulty chip and all the other information we've gathered so far.

"Over the next ninety minutes, review the information pertaining to the chip issue, and determine how to solve it in relation to your subgroup's role. Think about the application of all seven cornerstones as you go through the process. That includes incorporating periodic stones checks."

"What's a stones check?" asked Samantha.

"Ah, good question, Samantha," said Jason. "That's why we provided each of you the physical stones and an app to access them on your phone if you prefer. A stones check is when the group assesses how well the cornerstones are being applied, and we'll show you how that process works," explained Jason.

"At a stones check, each team member selects the one stone they feel the team is doing well and the one stone they feel the team should focus on to improve overall team performance. Once everyone has made their selection, each person shares which stones they picked and why. This usually takes no more than five minutes. From that input, the team leader decides what the team or individuals should do differently moving forward. That could include actions that team should take, such as accessing missing resources or adding more detail to better clarify the goal. Once the decision or decisions have been made, the team gets back to the job at hand. Make sense?" asked Jason.

Lots of head nods and yeses filled the room.

"Great! Let's give you a little pop quiz. If someone's effort is waning, what stone should the group check in with?"

"The dark blue one—Cornerstone 6: Consistent, United, and Enthusiastic Effort," said Samantha.

"That's correct," Jason said. "Now, what about if someone tries to circumvent the subgroups leader?"

"That's easy," said DeAngela. "Cornerstone 1: Leadership. The black stone."

"That's right," said Jason. "I think you all understand. What you also need to know is that in addition to regularly planning for stones checks to ensure the team is working to their optimum, anyone in the group at any time can call for a stones check. At this time, all other discussions are paused until there is team agreement about what steps to take to improve team performance based on the principles identified as needing attention as a result of what was shared in the stones check."

Jason next gave them a chance to practice the stones check process and then sent them off to work in their subgroups.

At two thirty, Gloria requested everyone's attention. "Jason and I are very impressed with your commitment to working to solve this problem and using the cornerstones consistently to do that.

"Now we are going to offer you another tool that you will use in conjunction with the seven cornerstones. Are you all ready for a mind-bending experience?"

Gloria and Jason broke the participants into groups of three, and within those groups, two people sat in back-to-back chairs and the third person stood beside those two chairs.

"While Jason hands out the materials to each group, I'm going to explain their purpose and everyone's role," began Gloria. "One of the seated individuals has a card with a tanagram image on it. We call this person the seated architect. The other seated person has a magnetic board and a variety of tanagram pieces. This is the builder. The seated architect's job is to help the builder recreate the image on the builder's board by verbally instructing them how to move their tanagrams around on the magnetic board, but because they are back to back, the seated architect is not allowed to see what the builder is doing. Everyone with me so far?"

There were several hesitant murmurs of "I think so."

"Now, the third person is called the standing architect. The standing architect stands beside the two chairs and can hear what is being said and see what is being done on the board but is not allowed to speak. So …

"The seated architect can speak but can't see what's going on.

"The standing architect can see what's going on but cannot speak.

"However, whenever they wish, the standing architect can tap the shoulder of the seated architect and trade places. The two architects can do this as frequently as they want. Any questions?"

Lots of concentrated faces shook their heads no.

"Okay, when I say go, each team will have ten minutes to recreate the image. "Ready, set, go!"

At minute seven, a few teams shouted, "Done!"

By the time Gloria called, "Stop!" all but one of the teams had completed the task.

"How did it feel doing that activity?" Jason asked the group.

"It was frustrating."

"I didn't get enough feedback to know if I was doing the right thing."

"I wanted to ask questions, but I wasn't sure if the builder was allowed to speak."

"I was the standing architect. When I saw it wasn't going right, I wanted to tap in, but I didn't want to offend the other architect. Finally it was getting so bad, I just had to jump in."

"That's all great feedback everyone—feedback that we want you to keep in mind as you move to round two and do it again. This time we're going to give you a different image to recreate, and you need to cut your time in half!" instructed Jason. "And yes, the builder can speak."

"Why didn't you tell us the builder could speak?" asked Dishant.

"Why didn't you ask?" said Jason with a smile. "Before you get started, discuss among your team what you can do differently to cut your time in half, and then we'll share your thinking." The groups came back with several ideas.

"We should tap in more often so that we get continuous feedback to keep it from going off the rails."

"We need a common language. When we say *triangle*, we need terminology to identify which triangle."

"And common language around how to place the tanagram pieces. We can't just say 'turn the rectangle'; we need to give it a specific direction, like one o'clock or north, south, or something like that, so we all know exactly what we mean."

"Fantastic ideas," said Jason. "Go!"

This time everyone was done within five minutes. Each team was successful in reducing its time, most of them by half, and was excited by its improvement. The team that had failed to succeed at all in the first round was particularly pleased. Everyone provided feedback on what made them faster this time and what could make them improve even more in the next round.

Once they'd had a chance to incorporate these ideas, Gloria challenged them to shorten their time even more and said, "Go!"

In the third round, every team completed the task in under three minutes. They were all amazed at how quickly and dramatically they improved. "Congratulations, everyone! That was fantastic. What did you all do differently that made you so much more successful?" asked Gloria.

"We weren't worried about offending someone, because every one of us was now focused on getting a better time," said the line tech.

"So," said Gloria, "the moment we added in an accountability to produce an improved result, you changed your behavior."

"I guess we did," said Gisela. "I think because we were all focused on the same goal, tapping in felt like a way in which I could help the team do better rather than offending the other person."

"And," said Gloria, "it sounded like each team was speaking the same language among themselves."

"Absolutely," said Sandy. "That made it so much less frustrating! It got me thinking about how to develop a true common language for my call center team. We think we have one, but this exercise has made me realize we really don't."

"Excellent insights, everyone. Now, let's talk about how to apply all that you've learned today to your chip problem," said Jason. "Remember, everybody at Talon Tech is going through this training, and as a result, everyone will understand and practice this behavior moving forward, so there is no excuse for not being sure of how to interact with your teammates. So, in regard to the chip problem, where can you tap in? Where should you tap in? What will keep you from tapping in? Why would it keep you from tapping in?"

A lively discussion ensued around how best to work together and solve the problem they were trying to resolve as a company and their part of the problem they were trying to solve as subgroups. Was it really a chip problem, or was it a customer service problem? To get a "ten bars of gold" result as quickly as possible, they all agreed on the following:

- Everyone should contribute whenever possible.

- Everyone should encourage their teammates to contribute.

- Every team must remain focused on the results they are trying to produce.

- A common language must be agreed upon and shared up front.

- The opportunity to tap in whenever possible must be encouraged.

"The Seven Cornerstones of Teamwork, the utilization of a common language, and the opportunity to tap in don't just apply to your chip problem," said Gloria. "They apply to everything you do. From this point forward, everyone at Talon Tech is expected to apply these principles and tools throughout their workday, every day. Do stones checks frequently as a great way to ensure you're tapping in.

"To help guide you with your stones checks, Jason has written the Five Laws of Cornerstones on the board."

1. *Every team member needs to bring their cornerstones to every team meeting.*

2. *The Seven Cornerstones of Teamwork should be used when people first meet to set up the team.*

3. *During team meetings, a stones check should be used at least once in the middle of the meeting. The team leader is responsible for this.*

4. *Cornerstones should be used at the end of the meeting by the team leader, who should call for a stones check and ask the following question: "When we next meet, what's the one area that we should try to improve upon?"*

5. *Anyone can call for a stones check at any time if they feel it will improve team performance.*

"Changing our behavior, even when we *want* to make the change, can be challenging. We understand that, and we will be here to support you as you learn to master these behaviors. Your leadership has committed to supporting you as you learn to consistently practice these behaviors, and you must commit to providing the same support to those you lead.

"Now you are equipped to resolve the chip problem with round-three efficiency instead of with round-one results!"

As Bridget prepared to head home that evening, she reflected on how pleased she was at how the training and tools were clearly helping to release the potential of her people, and she felt optimistic that her team would find a quicker and far better resolution to the chip problem than they would have six months ago.

However, as she headed for the parking garage, worry about the safety concerns and near misses in the distribution area began to occupy her thoughts. Just as Bridget reached her car, she slipped her hand into her pocket and gently bounced the bag of cornerstones residing there. "Lots of food for thought," she whispered to herself.

That evening, when the house had grown quiet, Bridget settled herself into the overstuffed chair on the porch. The air was crisp, and she wrapped her sweater around her a bit tighter. She gently shook the opened pouch onto the table and watched as the seven stones tumbled out. She studied them a bit and then opened her Transformation Notebook and put pen to paper:

1. *Model using the Seven Cornerstones of Teamwork for my team.*

2. *Use the cornerstones right from the outset to ensure the success of any new team.*

3. *Encourage "tapping in."*

4. *Establish a common language—always.*

5. *Ensure that everyone understands the message—leave no room for assumptions.*

THE PROOF OF
THE PUDDING

ou really do have a great view here, Bridget," said Natasha as she set two cups of steaming lattes and one tall, green smoothie onto the round conference table in the center of Bridget's expansive office.

"I know. I really try to take time to appreciate it every day, even if only for a few seconds," said Bridget, pulling her Transformation Notebook and a pen from her leather satchel tucked beneath her desk.

"Still writing in that thing, huh?" asked Marty as he plopped into a chair and rolled himself up to the table, reaching for the smoothie.

"Wow, didn't see that coming, Marty. You really are making some lifestyle changes."

"I'm trying."

"And yes, I'm still writing in my notebook," said Bridget as she joined her colleagues at the table and tapped one of the beads on her bracelet, illuminating the screen embedded in the table's center.

"Looks like we're getting right down to business," said Natasha, removing the cover from her coffee and gently blowing on its rising steam.

"Sorry, I do want to hear how everything's going with you two—I know we have some catching up to do—but I'm just too excited to show you my great news. Look!" Bridget said, pointing to the screen.

"Ah," said Natasha. "Pulse checks. I'm guessing you're getting some good feedback from employees."

"Yes," said Bridget excitedly, "and customer feedback, and …"

"Okay, okay," said Marty, laughing. "We get it—good results are coming in. Why don't you start with pulse checks and show us what you got."

"Okay," said Bridget. "Here are the survey questions we asked employees along with their responses."

On the screen was a list of four questions:

1. Do you feel that you are more engaged at Talon Tech than you were six months ago?

2. Do you feel you're better able to make a difference in your work at Talon Tech?

3. Do you feel that your leaders encourage you to speak up and add value?

4. Do you feel that you're better able to do your work now than you were three or five months ago?

The "yes" response rate of each followed:

1. 76 percent

2. 52 percent

3. 64 percent

4. 73 percent

"Impressive," said Marty.

"They are, right?" Bridget asked, looking back and forth between her friends for validation that she wasn't overestimating the success she was feeling.

"Yes," confirmed Natasha, "they are."

"Okay, good," said Bridget. "Obviously, still a lot of work to do, but I think we really are on the right track. Let me show you what I'm most excited about," she said, tapping the screen to pull up the next slide.

"Remember the chip issue I told you guys about"—Bridget looked at her watch—"just over two months ago?"

Natasha and Marty nodded.

"Well, this is the feedback from the customers impacted by the defective chips," said Bridget, directing them all back to the display screen.

1. Do you feel the problem you had was addressed to your satisfaction?

   - "Yes" response: 100 percent

   - "No" response: 0 percent

2. Were you given a reason for the issue and clarity on the steps taken by Talon Tech to keep it from reoccurring?

   - "Yes" response: 93 percent

   - "No" response: 7 percent

3. Do you feel you and your concerns were handled in a way that was courteous and professional?

   - "Yes" response: 95 percent

   - "No" response: 5 percent

4. Based on your overall experience with Talon Tech, will you continue to honor us with your business?

    □ "Yes" response: 98 percent

    □ "No" response: 2 percent

Marty whistled.

"As excited as I am about the metrics," Bridget began, "I'm more thrilled by the changes in behaviors I'm seeing across the organization. I saw the beginnings of the changes when the subgroups for the chip problem came together in the configurations training."

Bridget quickly flipped through her notebook, and when she landed on the page she wanted, she placed the palm of her hand on the fold to keep it open.

"When we first began tackling the customer service end of the chip issue utilizing the Seven Cornerstones of Teamwork, there was good discussion and some solid ideas generated. But after the configurations portion of the training, when we regrouped and began 'tapping in' and people kept interjecting with 'Is this a ten-bars-of-gold solution?' we brought it from an apology to the customer with an offer of either a full refund or replacement chip to 'Let's treat our customers in a way that makes them feel special.' In the end, we decided to incorporate a personal letter from a senior executive explaining not only that we were sorry but the reason the glitch occurred and what we were doing about it, and we guaranteed that we would follow through with our promise to resolve it to their satisfaction."

Bridget went on to explain that with team members at all levels having input into the process, everyone felt more accountable to follow up and follow through.

"We delivered what we promised and then followed up with a letter from a customer service lead with a thank-you for their patience.

All that garnered our much-improved customer service metrics and responses like"—Bridget skimmed the open page of her notebook—"'Thank you for your thoughtful communications while taking steps to resolve my issue. I'm sure it would have been easier to just refund me and be done with it. Two thumbs-up from me!' and 'You came through just like you said you would, and just in time for these dropping temperatures. Thank you.'" Bridget smiled. "I'm just going to read you one more, I promise. 'Talon Tech went above and beyond. I can't stop singing your praises.'"

Bridget leaned back in her chair. "I have to admit that I was still somewhat skeptical about whether or not the tools and behaviors we were all learning would actually be applied outside the controlled atmosphere of the training, but as you both know, Ray's training programs aren't typical—they're infectious!"

"They are," agreed Marty, "but even with the amazing level of enthusiasm they generate, they won't take hold if you don't keep reinforcing their application. Remember, they aren't magic. Ongoing model, coach, require from all leadership levels is essential."

"Oh, I see that, Marty," Bridget said. "In some ways, the magic is in the simplicity of it. I mean, the more I sit back and observe it in action, the more I see how logical it is and wonder why we did not know to do this before."

Marty and Natasha both nodded, laughing. "Marty and I have had this conversation," said Natasha. "We're just glad that once we saw the logic, its benefits, and how to continually implement it, we couldn't unsee it."

"Of course, challenges continue to occur. We had the beginnings of a safety issue at our distribution center in Chicago just as we were leaning into the chip issue, and I'm pleased to say that the team took control of it and resolved it quickly. In fact, I'm meeting with my

COO this afternoon to update me on what sounds like a positive resolution—even better, a resolution I wasn't involved in."

"And you're barely seven months in," said Marty. "Just wait until you're rounding up year two and all the behaviors are embedded throughout the organization—the results you get then will astound you."

"We're thirteen months in, and honestly—"

"Don't say it, Natasha," warned Marty.

"As I was saying," Natasha said, sending a frown Marty's way, "I honestly think we're ready to fly solo. In fact, I'm meeting with Ray next week to talk about how to gradually exit his team out over the next thirty days."

Marty shook his head and turned to Bridget. "Promise me you will not follow in her footsteps." And then, turning to Natasha, he said, "Mark my words—if you exit early, the transformation you have been working so hard on will not take hold. New behaviors take time and reinforcement to become habitual—there's simply no way around that."

"Well," said Bridget, pushing back her chair and standing up. "As much as I'd love to see how this conversation unfolds, I'm afraid I need to ask you to unfold it somewhere else, because I have to finish up a few things before heading to our recognition luncheon."

"We see how it is," needled Natasha as she and Marty gathered their coats and drinks. "She monopolizes the conversation with all her good news and then gives us the boot."

Bridget couldn't help but laugh out loud. "I did just do that, didn't I? Send me dates when you can both get together for a round of golf in the next couple of weeks, and I promise I will be all ears."

Gail, the head of Talon Tech's in-house events, met Bridget at the entrance to the large conference room that had been set up for the recognition luncheon. "This looks amazing, Gail," said Bridget.

"Yes, the events and facilities teams really outdid themselves. And," she said conspiratorially, "Jason is going to unveil a new technology tool we can begin utilizing throughout Talon Tech to further enhance our people-first initiative."

"Is he, now?" Bridget asked with a smile. Ray had shared the app with Bridget and her executive team a few weeks ago, and they were finding it invaluable. In fact, some of the executives couldn't wait for the big reveal before implementing URVU with a few of their direct reports.

Jordan had shared with the team just last week how her senior VP of logistics was surprised by the feedback he had received from one of his direct reports using this tool.

"They had talked about an issue they had disagreed upon," Jordan had explained, "but by the end of the discussion, my senior VP had been persuaded by his direct report and agreed with her proposed course of action. After they hung up, he sent her a URVU request for feedback under two topics. The first was Listening Well, which included feedback on 1. Didn't interrupt, 2. Asked questions, and 3. Paid attention. The second topic was Collaborative Approach, which included feedback on 1. Considered other opinions, 2. Shared personal thinking, 3. Promoted good discussion."

"I'm guessing the scores were high, since he agreed with her in the end," Tyler had said.

"You would think," had been Jordan's response, "but while he received fours and fives on not interrupting, asking questions, paying attention, and sharing personal thinking—which was great—he received only threes for considering other opinions and promoting good discussion."

"But he agreed with her," Tyler had restated. "That doesn't make sense."

"When he went back to discuss her feedback in person, she had told him that while he had agreed with her, she felt like she had had to really push for him to seriously consider her opinions. That he had kept circling the discussion back to why his made more sense than hers rather than having a balanced dialogue about the potential for both options."

"Well, now, that does make sense," Tyler had said.

"Yeah, I think we've all felt that way at one time or another," Harry had chimed in. "Some of my direct reports have also received feedback that's surprised them."

"The key is, what are they doing with that feedback?" Bridget had said as she looked toward Jordan and Harry.

"Took action on it. In talking through it with me, my SVP immediately saw it as an opportunity for him to improve his collaboration skills. He thanked his team member for her feedback, and they've engaged in more open communication on how she is moving forward on the project they had discussed."

Harry had nodded in agreement. "Similar response from all but one of my direct reports. She's just not taking the feedback as objectively as she needs to, which is feedback for me to improve my model, coach, and require techniques."

Bridget had shared with the group that she knew it was challenging to ask for and receive feedback and lauded them for their continued efforts. "The more consistently we access available feedback and act upon it, the more confident everyone will feel sharing it, and the more useful the knowledge we gather," Bridget had concluded.

Coming into a now-full conference room, Bridget took her seat as DeAngela stepped up to the podium.

"Good morning, everyone," DeAngela nearly shouted.

"Good morning!" the room boomed back.

"For those of you who don't know me, I'm DeAngela Jones, chief operations officer here at Talon Tech, and I am so excited to be here with you all today. I'm so proud of the results we are reaping from all your hard work these past few months." DeAngela tapped a bead on her bracelet, and on the screen behind her began to flow the many positive reviews they had received from their response to the chip issue.

"These rave reviews are in direct response to your efforts. That's right," said DeAngela amid the growing round of applause. "Stand up and give yourselves a round of applause."

Everyone jumped to their feet and began clapping. Bridget caught Ray's eye as he stood in the doorway and gave him a thumbs-up, which he returned with a smile and then ducked out of the conference room.

As the applause quieted and everyone took their seats, DeAngela continued.

"Everyone in this room has contributed to the success of our people-first initiative, and I thank each and every one of you. Today, I'd like to put a spotlight on those individuals who went above and beyond in resolving our chip issue, an issue that required the collaboration of cross-functional teams. When I call your name, please join me on the stage."

DeAngela called individuals from several areas of the company, including procurement, quality, manufacturing, technology, and customer service. Once they were all standing with her, DeAngela began, "It is my honor to recognize these individuals for their effective engagement of the Seven Cornerstones of Teamwork, for their willingness to tap in, and for the courage to keep reaching for ten bars of gold as they collaborated to find a solution for the chip issue." DeAngela turned her palms upward and began to wave both arms up and down, "That's right, you can all get clapping again. You know I'm not going to stop you."

As the applause quieted once again, DeAngela said, "Now, I would ask that Sandy, Steve, and Carlos step forward, please." DeAngela turned to face them. "Sandy, Steve, and Carlos, in addition to your collaboration efforts, it is my honor to recognize your initiative in identifying the opportunity to replicate the quality review steps taken to resolve the chip issue into best practices across all of manufacturing."

"Keep the applause coming," said DeAngela once again, laughing and waving her arms up and down, encouraging the audience.

Once those individuals returned to their seats, VP-level leaders took their turns at the podium to call upon and recognize the performance of individual members of their teams. After several more rounds of applause, the recognitions drew to a close. As lunch was being served, Jason jogged up the steps to the stage and called for everyone's attention. "What's URVU?" he asked.

That drew murmurs of confusion from the audience. "Our view of what?" someone called out. Bridget couldn't help but smile at the fun Jason was clearly having.

"URVU is an app we can all use to get immediate feedback from one another in real time," said Jason. As the screen filled with the URVU logo, Jason began to demonstrate how useful this tool could be to everyone at Talon Tech. Other than the sound of an occasional utensil clinking against a plate, the room was quiet as the audience absorbed all the possibilities that URVU offered to improve the quality of everyone's contributions. Just as dessert trays of petite pastries were being set on each table and coffee was being served, Bridget excused herself and headed back to her office to prepare for her three o'clock meeting with DeAngela and her health and safety director, Randy.

"Hey, DeAngela and Randy," Bridget said, motioning for them to take a seat at the conference table in her office. "DeAngela, you and your team outdid yourself with the recognition luncheon. It was impressive."

"Thanks," said DeAngela. "I was pretty happy with it. Now my team and I will get to work maximizing the energy and enthusiasm it generated."

"Good to see you, Randy," Bridget said. "Thanks for flying in, and congratulations on your recognition this afternoon. DeAngela tells me you took the lead to solve the accidents and near misses before they got beyond a 3 percent increase last month."

"I did," said Randy as he tapped a bead on his bracelet and cast an image onto the whiteboard. "But the results that show on this chart were truly a team effort. You can see that we had the slightest uptick of 0.5 percent in accidents and 1 percent in near misses about a month ago."

"I remember," said Bridget, "We were just kicking the chip resolution into high gear."

"Right," said Randy. "We monitored it closely for a couple of weeks while I began to inquire with some of the 'old men' of the company, like the maintenance crews and drivers, to start to gather some information in case it wasn't an anomaly we were seeing."

"Looks like at the end of those couple of weeks, it did start to tick up a bit," said Bridget.

"It did," said Randy. "At that point we had a 1.5 percent rate of accidents and a 2 percent rate of near misses. When I met with DeAngela to share the insights I had gathered, we walked through the cornerstones and configurations training she had been through and how they had applied it to the chip issue."

"And," said DeAngela, "I bumped Randy up the line so he could get into the training the following week."

"Right," said Randy, "and DeAngela and I worked quickly to determine who the members of the subgroups needed to be and found two members who hadn't had the training yet either, so they took it with me. Once we were all up to speed, it really was amazing how well we were all able to collaborate and find the root cause and resolution quickly. To be honest, I'd never experienced anything quite like it."

Randy went on to explain the makeup of the cross-functional team for which he served as the Black Stone Leader and the three subgroups of that team. "With manufacturing as part of the team, we were able to get to the root of the problem quickly—a significant increase in orders going out the door seemingly overnight."

Anticipating Bridget's question, DeAngela explained that Smart Tech had dropped one of its products, and their customers were turning to Talon Tech to fill that void.

"Did nobody see this coming?" asked Bridget.

"I didn't, and neither did anyone on my team. Seems they kept it under wraps well," said DeAngela.

Bridget turned back to Randy. "Sorry, Randy. Please continue."

"Once we determined the cause, I continued to model the use of the cornerstones consistently, and by the third meeting, everyone was using the cornerstones principles and stone checks unprompted. Within a week, we had a solution for the driver shortage and the additional resources maintenance needed to move forward."

"See that dip to below 1 percent in both near misses and accidents less than five days after the peak?" DeAngela asked Bridget.

"Yes. Impressive," said Bridget.

"That's a result of Randy's leadership, and he's determined to get it to zero!"

Once the meeting had concluded and Bridget was once again alone in the quiet of her office, she couldn't shake the feeling that something wasn't right. Why hadn't her CIO or CRO known about the potential influx of sales? She looked at her watch. It was almost four thirty. "Looks like I'm not going to be home by six," she said to herself with a sigh as she sent an urgent message to Andrea and Gisela to meet in her office in fifteen minutes and then gave Rob a quick call to let him know that he and the kids should start dinner without her.

She turned to face the churning river below. Taking a few deep breaths, she reminded herself of the many positives that had occurred today.

"What's all the urgency, Bridget?" Andrea asked as she walked into Bridget's office with Gisela close behind.

"Have a seat and I'll explain," she said, motioning to the chairs in front of her desk. "Clearly, Smart Tech was keeping the discontinuation of their product under wraps until they were ready to pull the plug, but still, as Talon Tech's CIO and CRO, one or both of you should have heard some whispers of it."

"It was a bit of a surprise," said Gisela. "But I'm definitely not complaining, and neither is anyone on my team. An increase in sales is always good news!"

"Yes and no," said Bridget. "There's the obvious positive increase in revenue, but operations was wholly unprepared, and that lack of preparedness put undue pressure on distribution."

"Now that I think about it," said Gisela as she turned to Andrea, "I did mention to you a few months ago that I heard some very low-level rumors about Smart Tech adjusting its product line. But you said you already knew about it, and—"

Andrea cut her off. "Oh, please," she said. "The increase is great news, and logistics delivered. I don't know why we're even talking about this."

Bridget looked at Gisela. "Gisela, I'm sorry I took up your time unnecessarily. Please go and enjoy the rest of your evening."

Once Gisela had left the office, Bridget turned to Andrea. "So," Bridget said, fighting to keep a measured tone, "let me get this straight. You, the chief information officer for this company, knew, and you *chose* not to prepare operations for the additional work?"

"It's an increase, Bridget. Let's take the win—we need it," Andrea said flatly. "Can I go home and enjoy my evening, too?"

Bridget slapped her palm on the table. Andrea jumped.

"That mindset and behavior, Andrea, is how we got into the problem in the first place. We had executives and people making decisions without considering the implications for the organization and, more importantly, the implications for our people. Your decision not to share it has put people's health and safety at risk.

"The people-first initiative is how we are setting Talon Tech back on a path of success. If you had been following the teachings and trainings of the initiative—something you have been resisting from the start—you would have sought some input on this decision. You could have brought a group of people together and said, 'Listen, I'm going to be the Black Stone Leader here, but this is what I'm hearing. What do you think?' And from that, you would've garnered the wisdom and insight of the very people who make it happen, and it still would have remained your decision to make. That's how we build an empowered organization capable of producing a ten-bar-of-gold outcome that is effective, efficient, *and* safe.

"But once again, you have demonstrated your lack of commitment to harnessing the power of our people. Once again, you have chosen to focus only on what matters to you."

"This is ridiculous," Andrea sputtered.

"You're right, Andrea. It is, and your unwillingness to respect what others can contribute and to gather the information necessary has put people's safety at risk and left us picking up the pieces of your uninformed decision when we could have been ahead of the curve and profiting greatly. Your services are no longer needed at Talon Tech."

WEATHERING
THE STORM

"I followed Andrea to her office and demanded she hand over all her Talon Tech devices," Bridget told Ray when he arrived in her office in response to her call. "She was too stunned to not comply." Bridget shook her head in disbelief. "Then I called the head of security while she was standing there and had them shut down her access to any and all devices, hardware, and facilities. Then"—Bridget paused to take a breath—"I walked her out the door myself."

Ray leaned back in his chair and let out a sigh. "Wow. Looks like DeAngela was right. Andrea was on a warpath about something."

"But Andrea is always on a warpath about something, and many times her fierce resolve to do what's right for the company has saved us. But I guess once she lost faith in me, once she saw Talon Tech begin to slide under my watch—albeit a very short-lived slide—she could no longer see the forest for the trees."

"Even when it was obvious Talon Tech was starting to turn around."

"Well, my idea of turning things around and Andrea's clearly weren't aligned. Her laser focus certainly has its place in advancing technologies, but it's so clear to me now that if we had continued down that path, Talon Tech's slide would have been a long one. One we may not have recovered from. And"—by this point, Bridget had to laugh—"it turns out she had the inside scoop about Smart Tech's product discontinuation because she had been trying to convince its CIO that my board would be giving me the boot soon, and she wanted him to come in as Talon Tech's new CEO."

"I know I already said this, but wow! Do you think its CIO discontinued that product on purpose?"

"Wow is right, and no, I don't think so," said Bridget. "He's since moved on to another tech company. It will be interesting to see what happens with Smart Tech."

"I sense there is more than a passing interest in that observation?" questioned Ray.

"It is Talon Tech's closest competitor—they just aren't as good as us," Bridget said with a smile. "A potential acquisition has been in the back of my mind for quite some time, but I haven't felt confident we could handle it. But if we keep making inroads with our people-first initiative, who knows …" Bridget glanced at her watch. "I can't believe how late it is. I do appreciate your responding to my call so quickly."

"Of course. Clearly you handled the surprise and its fallout well, but it does always help to talk through it with someone else to make sure you've covered all the bases."

"I should have seen this and gotten ahead of it," Bridget said. "Andrea didn't come right out and say it, but I got the impression that she had one or two direct reports who were supporting her course of action, which we'll also have to address."

"We have some work to do, for sure. We'll lay out what that looks like at the executive leadership team tomorrow morning."

"Ugh," said Bridget as she stood up and began to get herself organized to go.

"What's wrong?" asked Ray, shrugging on his coat.

"It's now just dawning on me that I need to find a replacement CIO ASAP!"

"You have plenty of time to begin to sort that out tomorrow. Tonight, try to relax with Rob and the kids. I'll see you at the leadership meeting in the morning," said Ray as he left Bridget's office and headed for the elevators.

The kids were in bed when Bridget arrived home, and she tiptoed into each of their rooms to check on them. As usual, Craig was lying on his back, sleeping peacefully, blankets tucked in tightly around him. Maddie, on the other hand, looked like she had just fought off a tiger, her arms and legs spread every which way and the blankets a tangled mess. Bridget did her best to untangle her daughter without waking her.

"How was dinner?" Bridget asked as she headed into the kitchen and gave Rob a quick kiss on the cheek.

"Gotta say, it was pretty good for burgers and a side of boxed mac and cheese," said Rob, removing her plate from the oven.

"Sounds like just the comfort food I need tonight." Bridget eagerly grabbed the plate along with utensils and napkin and headed straight for the couch. Once comfortably settled, she scooped up a forkful of mac and cheese and began to eat. She was hungrier than she realized. Once she had eaten half her dinner, she paused to fill Rob in on Andrea and the ensuing repercussions. He was as surprised as Bridget had been and agreed that she had done the right thing in ushering Andrea out the door immediately.

Bridget left the house early the next morning and headed to the gym. She had let her commitment to working out lapse these past couple of months, and it was time to recommit to the level of the pig in a bacon-and-egg breakfast starting today. Twenty minutes of rowing and twenty minutes of weights gave her time to release stress and clear her mind for what was sure to be a grueling day. After a quick shower, she stopped by the campus cafeteria for a smoothie before heading to her office.

Nick arrived a few minutes later and gave her an update on her schedule for the day.

"Thanks, Nick. I anticipate my nine-thirty meeting will last at least a couple of hours. During that time, I want no interruptions unless the building is on fire."

"You got it, Bridget," said Nick before heading back to his desk.

Bridget sat at the head of the large conference table, making last-minute notes to the agenda. She looked at her watch. *Ten minutes until the proverbial damn bursts*, she thought just as Gisela walked in.

"Good morning, or should I just say morning?" asked Gisela as she walked over to the side table and poured herself a glass of lemon water.

"Just morning will do," replied Bridget with a faltering smile.

"So," said Gisela, settling into a chair near Bridget. "What in the world was that all about?"

"What in the world, indeed," said Bridget. "You'll hear all about it in just a couple of minutes," Bridget promised as she welcomed incoming team members. "It's the first item on my agenda."

"Good morning, everyone," Bridget began once everyone was seated. "Now that you are all here, I have some very recent news to share." Bridget paused a moment.

DeAngela grew impatient. "Please just spit it out, Bridget. We all know something big is going on with Andrea. We just don't know what."

DeAngela's insistence reminded her that the people around this table were a cohesive unit. They were a much stronger team than they had been just a few months ago. They would weather this storm. "Okay," said Bridget. "Here's what's happened." Much the same way she had with Ray last night, she walked her team through the drama that had unfolded and Andrea's abrupt departure from all things Talon Tech.

"I take full responsibility for the situation. Clearly I was not paying the level of attention I should have," said Bridget. "While we have made tremendous progress these last seven months, there is still work to do. And as always, the work begins with everyone in this room. Anyone have any questions before we get started?"

"Not a question," said Gisela. "I just want to thank you for sharing the full story with us." There were nods in agreement from around the table.

"Thank you, Gisela. Anyone else?"

"We'll get through this, Bridget," said Jordan. And then with a wink and a nod at Ray, she said, "We all weathered the Ray storm." That elicited chortles from around the table. "We'll weather this storm, too."

"Then let's get to work," said Ray with a grin. "First, we are going to get our messaging aligned, which will be guided by marketing and HR. Samantha and Harry, if you two could meet with Bridget and me immediately following this meeting?"

"I can do that," said Samantha, tapping her watch and making the necessary adjustments to her calendar.

"Me too," said Harry.

"Great," said Bridget. "Operations, finance, and HR will all come into play as we delegate Andrea's responsibilities to her direct reports until we find her replacement. DeAngela, Dishant, and Harry—can the three of you meet with Ray and me at one o'clock?"

They all checked their schedules and nodded their assent.

"Good work, everyone. Before you go, I do want to share some positive news. You've all seen the great results from the pulse checks and the implementation of best practices. Now," Bridget said, looking up at the screen and tapping her bracelet, "I want to show you the end-of-quarter numbers I pulled this morning."

"Ooh," said Gisela. "I bet the board likes those numbers. I know I do."

"They will," said Bridget, "once I share them with them. But I wanted you all to be the first to see the increase in retention, which has led to increases in both productivity and profitability that you have all worked so hard to achieve. While I do want these numbers to climb higher," she said with a laugh, "the tremendous progress we have made is thanks to each and every one of you. Thank you for trusting me and for committing to the people-first initiative."

Then she turned to Harry and DeAngela. "Let's get time on the books next week to talk about plans to recognize our leaders and employees for these great results."

Once the meeting concluded, Bridget, Ray, Samantha, and Harry spent the next hour walking through messaging options that were honest but did not offer more detail than was necessary. As part of their commitment to putting people first, they realized the importance of great and transparent communication.

It was agreed that Bridget would convene a meeting with Andrea's direct reports first thing tomorrow morning. Luck had been on her side with timing. Andrea had been scheduled to be in the London office for the next few days, so she had had Andrea's assistant inform that office that she would need to reschedule and then put an out-of-

office reply on Andrea's email. Bridget couldn't be sure if Andrea had reached out to those she was closest to here at Talon Tech, but she could only control so much.

Once they had tied down the messaging, they moved on to communication strategy and execution.

Samantha looked at Bridget. "Just want to confirm that everything is ready for this to go out tomorrow morning at ten."

"Yes," said Bridget. "Tyler and I spoke early this morning. He's getting legalities in order as we speak. I'm addressing Andrea's direct reports at nine, and once that concludes, you'll execute the messaging."

Bridget looked at Ray and Harry. "Looks like we have time for a quick lunch before our one o'clock with DeAngela and Dishant." Then she turned to Samantha. "Care to join us for a bite to eat in the cafeteria, Sam?"

"Thanks, Bridget, but before I head to lunch, I'm going to get working on all this while it's fresh in my mind."

"Okay. Thanks for your help. I know this wasn't how you planned to spend your morning," said Bridget. "And Harry, I know I'm already monopolizing so much of your time today, but HR's role in all this is critical. Can you also meet with Ray and me as soon as we conclude our one o'clock to start mapping out the recruitment plan for our next CIO? I'm choosing to see this as an opportunity to revamp our recruiting practices to ensure we are hiring people who not only have the skills we are looking for but who are aligned with our new behaviors and culture."

"You got it," said Harry. "Shall we go, before we lose our small window for lunch?"

Once they stepped outside, they all agreed the weather was too nice to eat in the cafeteria, so they grabbed their sandwiches and drinks and sat at one of the picnic tables in the center of the campus courtyard.

"I think today is a dessert-first kind of day," said Bridget as she peeled the top off the paper cup and skimmed her small wooden spoon across the top of the softening strawberry ice cream.

"You look like a little kid," said Harry, laughing.

"If only I could be one for a day," sighed Bridget.

"Right," said Harry. "Summer camp starts next week, and when my kids excitedly tell me all the great things they are going to do, I have to admit, I'm jealous. I want to go to camp, too!"

"That just gave me an idea," said Bridget as she began typing away on her phone. "I'm texting DeAngela and Dishant to meet us out here for our one o'clock instead of returning to the conference room. You both good with that?" she asked, looking up.

Harry and Ray both gave her a thumbs-up.

Bridget was glad she had thought of moving the meeting outdoors. It had given them all a renewed energy that had resulted in a highly productive meeting. While challenges related to Andrea's abrupt departure still lay ahead, Bridget felt good about how the day had unfolded. Tomorrow morning's company-wide messaging would go out, marketing and HR were firing up all cylinders in their search for Talon Tech's new CIO, and her leadership team had all bases covered until that person was found.

After the meeting had ended and they had all left, Bridget took advantage of having a few moments alone to write in her Transformation Notebook:

Remember the Six Areas of Focus:
- *Leadership: Each of us must own the outcome for this initiative and hold people accountable for modeling the new behaviors.*

- *Communication: Let everyone know continually and consistently how we are doing things and why. This must be intentional and planned for.*

- *Alignment: Align all the human resource practices. This shift in how we're leading our people must touch every aspect of what HR is responsible for.*

- *Training: Experiential training. First train leaders at all levels; then train all employees. Be sure the training links to our real-world issues.*

- *Reinforcement: Provide support and activities to ensure that the training sticks. These must be led by our line managers.*

- *Metrics: Continuous measurement of progress/outcomes. Share these with everyone.*

Bridget knew she could flip back to one of her first entries in her notebook and find this same list, but she felt it was important to write it again now that she understood their importance and how necessary they *all* were for a successful transformation and her increased understanding of them.

ARE WE
THERE YET?

ell, you look like the cat that ate the canary," said Bridget when Harry sauntered into her office and took a seat, a big smile spreading across his face.

"Grace accepted the position."

"Fantastic," said Bridget. "Sounds like everyone on the leadership team feels the same way you and I do about Talon Tech's new CIO."

"Oh, yes," said Harry. "Everyone agreed she'll be a great fit. I know that after having the position vacant for the last ten weeks, everyone is anxious to have her start ASAP, but Grace's timeline is four weeks."

"While I know the vacancy has stretched everyone, we did agree from the beginning we wouldn't rush the process and would wait for the right person to fill Andrea's position," Bridget assured Harry. "Honestly, it's provided the time we needed to make sure everyone on the technology side was fully committed to the people-first initiative and there were no remaining Andrea holdouts."

"That's true," said Harry. "Grace will be immersed into Talon Tech's people-first culture on day one."

"You'll let the leadership team and Ray know?"

"I will," said Harry.

"I'm so proud," said Bridget, "of how everyone has stepped up during this time of transition *and* continued full steam ahead on our initiative. You've played a significant role in our positive momentum and success, Harry, and I truly appreciate your dedication and contributions."

The news that Talon Tech would have a new CIO by the end of next month was the perfect ending to Bridget's day. *We got this*, she thought as she pulled out of Talon Tech's parking lot and headed to her dinner date with her husband.

Rob had arrived before her and was already sitting in what they had come to think of as *their* booth in their favorite pizza place. The waiter was just setting down a big bowl of salad along with a glass of cold root beer for each of them when Bridget arrived at the table.

Once Bridget was settled, Rob raised his glass and said, "Here's to successfully navigating another school year!"

"We did it!" said Bridget.

"I suppose," said Rob with a laugh, "we should give some credit to Craig and Maddie for their success. I'm sure they'll enjoy their sleepover with Tamara and Devon tonight."

"To Craig and Maddie," Bridget cheered, clinking Rob's glass for a second time.

Over salad and appetizers, they talked about summer plans and how quickly the next school year would be here and what the new grade levels would mean for their son and daughter. By the time their pizza arrived, Rob said, "Okay, spill it. You haven't even mentioned work, and I can tell you're ruminating on something."

"All good at work. Exceptionally good, actually. Harry just hired our new CIO. She starts next month."

Rob paused, waiting for more. When Bridget didn't elaborate, he said, "But …"

Bridget set her fork down and looked at Rob. "Well, you know Natasha moved on without Ray and his team a couple of months ago."

"Yes," said Rob slowly.

"Well, she says that so far they are successfully continuing their transformation trajectory—all metrics continue to be strong. Our metrics continue to head in the right direction, too—the board is happy, and our teams are jumping on potential problems and solving them before they become real problems."

"And?" asked Rob.

"Well, even abruptly losing our CIO and the position being vacant for a bit hasn't thrown any of the leadership team off their game. They have all stepped up to a whole new level, and now the position will be filled in just a few weeks."

"Did Ray assist with the plan to move forward after Andrea's departure?"

"I see what you're doing," said Bridget. "And yes, Ray helped guide us in the process, but now that he has, I feel like we'll be able to guide ourselves in these types of challenges as we move forward. Does it still make sense to invest that type of cost and time if we are able to continue on our own …" Bridget trailed off.

"Tempting to be sure," said Rob. "You have a healthy bottom line again, and you only want to make it healthier. What does Ray say?" When he saw the look on his wife's face, he sat back and smiled. "You haven't mentioned this to Ray yet."

"Not yet."

"Well, he's guided you incredibly well to this point. My suggestion would be to get his advice."

"I'm planning to in our meeting tomorrow," Bridget said as she pulled her Transformation Notebook from her bag and set it open on the table. "Right here is my first question for Ray: *Is Talon Tech ready for you to exit?*"

INDIA INK

"Good morning, Bridget," said Ray as he entered her office.

Bridget was already seated at the small conference table with her laptop and Transformation Notebook. "Good morning, Ray," she said with a smile. "You bring gifts, I see."

"Yes, iced tea this morning," he said as he placed the to-go cups on the table and took a seat.

"Perfect for this first day of summer heat. Thank you."

They both began to speak at once.

"Sorry," said Bridget. "We just have so much to talk about this morning that I'm eager to jump in."

Ray smiled. "We do have a lot to process today. If you wouldn't mind indulging me for a moment before we dig in, I'd like to tell you a story."

Bridget sat back, curious. "Of course. I'm listening."

"Okay," Ray began. "I'm standing in a meeting room holding a glass of water, and I spill the water on the carpet. It leaves a dark stain. The cleaning crew comes in that night to clean as usual, but the stain has vanished. So much so that unless someone told them they had spilt water on it, they would not know it. The water has evaporated.

"The next day, I'm in the meeting room and I spill a bottle of India ink on the carpet. It leaves a dark stain. That night when the cleaning crew comes in, the stain is still there. The crew attempts to remove it, but they're never going to get it out, because India ink embeds itself so thoroughly in the material that it cannot be removed.

"So, why am I telling you this story? When people go through a culture transformation and they reach the eight- to ten-month mark, they begin to see a meaningful impact. But that big dark splotch of impact they see is merely a water stain. A water stain that will evaporate if they do not stay the course and reinforce it and make sure everybody understands that this is the new way of behaving.

"For that impact to become India ink, to become part of an organization's DNA, they must encourage everyone in the organization to consistently apply the behaviors for two to three years. If an organization stops when it's still a water stain, complacency will set in, and the transformational culture will not take hold. Now, it may hold as long as that transformational CEO is in place, but as soon as that CEO leaves or moves on to concentrate on other priorities, so does the culture, because it has not yet become part of the organization's DNA. It is only when the culture is so powerfully ingrained in the company that people continue to embrace the culture regardless of its leader that the transformation is successful."

"Hmm," murmured Bridget as she sat back in her chair and eyed Ray. "Why this story today? Have you been speaking to my husband?"

Ray laughed and put his hand up in mock surrender. "No, I have not spoken to Rob. You and your team have had a lot of strong wins recently despite the upheaval of a vacant CIO position. All that builds momentum and confidence—which is great."

"But?"

"But it sometimes creates overconfidence that the behavior changes can withstand the test of time or change of leadership—that they are more than a water stain. If leaders are going to question whether to stay the course or not, they do so now."

Bridget was quiet for a moment. She fidgeted with a loose paper clip and then looked at Ray. "But it feels like we've really got this."

"It does," said Ray. "What you have is the beginnings of getting this. You also have tremendous confidence and momentum to help you stay the course. If you do, you'll reach the point of *knowing* you got this, because you will see it in action in every facet of the organization."

"You don't think it is in every facet yet?"

"I know it's not. But don't take my word for it. Let's test it with the Accountable Leader Loop, which is the next tool to be taught and applied. We meet with leadership this afternoon, don't we?"

"We do."

"Great. Let me walk you through the Accountable Leader Loop. It's a useful barometer of how embedded the culture truly is. You game?"

"Always," said Bridget, smiling and putting aside both her notebook and her question for Ray about whether Talon Tech was ready to move forward on its own. *Let's see how the afternoon leadership session plays out first*, she thought.

After her meeting with Ray, Bridget met with Tyler and Dishant to do a preliminary legal and financial review of what it would mean to acquire Smart Tech. If Talon Tech was ready for an acquisition in the near future, she wanted to know what her options were.

At three o'clock, the leadership team was gathered in the conference room. Bridget welcomed everyone, addressed the items on their weekly leadership agenda, and then handed the reins over to Ray.

"Thank you, Bridget," Ray said as he walked over to the white-board and wrote three questions.

1. *How can I best support the application of the new behaviors?*

2. *What feedback are you receiving about their implementation and impact?*

3. *What action have you taken as a result?*

"For the rest of this meeting, we are going to focus on making sure we are fully implementing what's called the Accountable Leader Loop up and down the leadership ladder. But before we do that, I want to tell you a story about a leader who truly understood accountability," he said, rejoining them at the table.

"A few years ago, I was engaged to speak to a group of global executives who were running sales functions. The presentation was focused on accountability. So, we asked the participants to come prepared with various examples of what it meant to be accountable. One executive leading a sales team in South America shared his accountability story. There had been an earthquake, and the stores they were selling their product into were devastated—it would be weeks before they would be up and running again. The executive's initial thought was to inform the head office that as a result of the earthquake's devastation, he was going to miss his targets that quarter. Seems a reasonable response, right?" Ray asked the group. There were vigorous head nods around the table.

"Instead, he determined it was his job to deliver on his commitments, so he decided to first bring his team together and ask what they felt they could do to meet their targets within the reality they were facing. The team decided they would initiate steps to sell the product well outside the earthquake zone, which was also outside their normal sales areas. They then went and created new customer and distribution channels and met their numbers for the quarter."

"Wow," said Gisela. "That is unbelievable."

"It is," said Ray. "And they also helped the stores that had suffered from the earthquake get back on their feet. The outcome of that presentation was 'If you commit, you've got to deliver. No excuses.'"

Ray returned to the whiteboard. "Now, the first step in any commitment," he said as he wrote, "is understanding, discussing, and agreeing to what you are committing to. The second step is ensuring that you have the capabilities to deliver on that commitment." He turned to face the group. "Only when those two parts are in place can one truly commit."

"Right," said Tyler. "That's where the decision-making model comes into play to help ensure that what's being asked for is achievable, that we understand what the person or team believes they need to fulfill that commitment, and that we provide them the necessary resources to make it happen."

"And the sandbox," Jordan chimed in., "Establishing how much freedom to act a leader should be given so that they can deliver on their commitment."

"And the parameters of that sandbox are going to continually adapt to the person's capabilities to get the job done," Tyler added.

"Exactly," said Ray. "Now, go back to the questions I wrote on the board earlier," he said, drawing a circle around them.

1. *How can I best support the application of the new behaviors?*

2. *What feedback are you receiving about their implementation and impact?*

3. *What action have you taken as a result?*

Over the next hour, Bridget and her team answered Ray's three questions. Their responses indicated gaps. While they were all accessing most of the tools and taking action as needed, they weren't always doing so consistently. They all recommitted to putting them into practice in every applicable circumstance. As they delved into how far down the ladder this degree of accountability was reaching, they were dismayed to discover that most of them weren't sure beyond the director level. Ray could feel the team's concern.

"I'm glad you're concerned with what we've just discovered," he said.

"Gee, thanks," quipped Jordan.

"Let me explain. Not knowing how far down the Accountability Leader Loop is reaching is unsatisfactory to be sure, but that you're concerned about it reaffirms for me that you understand the importance of every leader being personally accountable for releasing the potential of their team members. And don't be too discouraged. The transformation you have made these past ten months has been tremendous. From the beginning, I was clear that this transformation was a long game, and to be as far as you are before half-time is honestly impressive. Let's do this," said Ray. "Over the next two weeks, you all go back and see how far down the accountability loop has reached in your functional area, and then we'll reconvene to review the data you've gathered. Let's call it a morning."

Two weeks later, the leadership team was once again gathered in the conference room. "Good to see everyone," said Ray once everyone was settled. "Now," he said pointing to the whiteboard, "how'd everyone do with the three questions?"

"So," began DeAngela, "all directors in operations reported that the Accountable Leader Loop was reaching the lowest management level. Issues were coming up, but all were addressed quickly because questions and issues were discussed in real time."

"That's great," said Ray.

"It was until the call center in Nevada. Turns out every cross-functional team they put together quickly fell apart, so they stopped trying."

"Were you able to figure out why?" asked Ray.

"Yes, they were having trouble identifying the decision maker, and with no leader, chaos reigned. The reason they had trouble with this centered around confusion as to the level of freedom they had to act."

"So, now what?" asked Ray.

"Well, the director did a review of the training and walked the manager through the role of the Black Stone Leader and the process for determining who that person should be. She let him know that whenever he is uncertain, he should come to her, and she'll provide him with guidance."

"Super, and the director is going to continue to check in," said Ray.

"Oh, yes," said DeAngela.

Jordan jumped in. "We had a few areas that weren't reaching all the way to the manager level, but now that they've begun doing so, the issues that are arising have been easily addressed … except one."

"What's that?" asked Ray.

"The manufacturing plant in Oklahoma. The line manager knows his communication needs to be effective and frequent, but he's not a natural communicator, so he has no idea how to go about it. He hadn't been asked about it, so it just kind of fell by the wayside."

"How's it being addressed?" asked Ray.

"Honestly, I was hoping you could give me some guidance. Do we send him to a communications course? I'm not even sure what that type of course would look like."

"I had a couple of areas lacking communication skills as well," Tyler chimed in.

"Okay," Ray said. "My team will run our communications course for them next week. It's super practical and will help a lot. If you then find that one of them needs something more, let me know."

They continued around the table until each member of the leadership team had shared the results of their Accountable Leader Loop and the gaps they had uncovered. The good news was that all were resolvable now that everyone was consistently being held accountable. The biggest surprise came when one of the managers under Dishant's purview didn't know what the cornerstones were. Turns out she had been promoted in the midst of the training and just hadn't been able to retain and put all the training into practice while also learning her new responsibilities. Dishant explained that her direct supervisor was training her and her entire team in a cornerstone refresher course.

"I'm so pleased with these results," said Ray.

"I am, too," said Bridget. She confessed to her team that she had been considering moving forward without Ray's assistance. "But this exercise," she continued, "has shown me that our people-first initiative is not fully embedded in the organization—yet. But it has also demonstrated how far we've come in less than a year, and it has left no doubt that we will achieve India ink by the end of next year."

That garnered several confused looks. "India what?" asked Harry.

Bridget looked to Ray.

"I think you should tell the story, Bridget," said Ray.

Later that evening, with the dishes done and the kids in bed, Bridget found her way, once again, to the overstuffed chair on the porch. Comforted by the serenading crickets and warm summer breeze, she opened her Transformation Notebook:

Stay the course even when it seems impossible—I mean it!

Bridget had made that note more than once, but she had now experienced how tempting it could be to mistake a water stain for India ink, and she was determined not to fall for the illusion.

And remember, it's not magic—the process is foolproof if you follow it:

1. *Our executives are trained to model, coach, and require the new behavior.*

2. *Our leaders are trained to model, coach, and require the new behavior.*

3. *Our employees are trained on the new behavior and understand that their leader is there to coach them on those behaviors.*

4. *We employ the Accountable Leader Loop consistently:*

   □ *Commit to putting the new behaviors into practice in every applicable circumstance.*

   □ *Test it regularly to make sure the loop is reaching every level.*

5. *Our human resources processes and policies are tied to our people-first initiative:*

   □ *We promote people who demonstrate the new behavior.*

   □ *We hire people who have an inclination toward the new behavior.*

6. *All our communications reinforce that the new behavior is the way to go.*

7. *We share our metrics that result from consistently practicing the new behavior.*

8. *If we consistently and continually follow this process, we will achieve ten bars of gold every time.*

LINE MANAGERS
TAKE THE STAGE

Almost a year into Talon Tech's people-first initiative, Bridget had fully regained her confidence as the CEO of a Fortune 100 global technology company. She felt fortunate that although her confidence may have faltered for a short period of time, she never lost her incredible passion and abilities for advancing technologies, and now, coupled with a deep understanding of how to harness the potential of her people, she felt unstoppable.

Sitting among her peers this morning in the ELO mastermind group and sharing how Talon Tech was now on a sure footing and continuing its transformational trajectory, she felt grateful to the group for sharing their wisdom and encouragement along the way, and she told them so.

"Time to grab a cup of coffee?" askcd Natasha as they headed to their cars after the meeting.

"I wish," said Bridget, leaning against her car.

"Okay, but before you go, I have to know what you decided about Ray. Certainly sounds like everything's humming along at Talon Tech," said Natasha.

Bridget smiled. "I know you want me to go rogue with you, Natasha, and I confess I almost did after our last conversation, but when I saw the power of the Accountable Leader Loop, it was clear that we're not where we need to be yet and that we still need Ray's guidance to make sure it sticks."

Natasha laughed. "You know I'd love to have a partner in crime, but the fact is, you know Talon Tech better than anyone, and you need to stick with what you feel is right. For me, an earlier exit for VGS Medical to move forward on our own felt right. Our HR department has been spearheading our initiative for almost five months now. Honestly, we're probably not running as smoothly as we were with Ray and his team, but we continue to consistently communicate the initiative, and HR is continuing to make it a priority."

"I get how tempting it is. I guess I've just really taken to heart Ray's refrain that our early successes need constant reinforcement for at least two years and that the reinforcement must go beyond just communication and messaging."

"That just doesn't seem to be necessary from my perspective," said Natasha. "We continue to make headway, and I don't see any reason why we can't continue on our current trajectory."

"Let's hope we've both chosen wisely for our organizations," Bridget said as she started her car with a tap to her bracelet.

The day went by in a blur of meetings, and before Bridget knew it, Nick was poking his head into her office to say good night.

"Goodnight, Nick," said Bridget. With the sound of the closing elevator doors, Bridget tapped a bead on her bracelet, and the hall lights dimmed. In the glow of her desk lamp, she pulled her Transformation Notebook from her desk drawer and made a couple of quick notes for the meeting she had scheduled with Ray and Harry in the morning. Her conversation with Natasha had gotten her thinking about whether the reinforcements they were employing beyond communication and messaging were enough.

> *Questions for Ray:*
> 1. *How do we ensure reinforcement of long-term behaviors beyond communication and messaging?*
> 2. *The Accountable Leader Loop reaches all levels of leadership, but are there additional things we can incorporate to support reinforcement at the line manager level?*

Bridget left her notebook open, ready for her meeting with Ray and Harry, and headed home for the night.

The next morning, traffic was unusually heavy on the way in to the office, and Bridget called Nick to let him know she would be a few minutes late and to please get Ray and Harry settled in her office when they arrived.

With her car finally parked, Bridget checked the time. *Not so late*, she thought. Just as she stepped into Talon Tech's lobby, DeAngela asked if she had a moment. "Only a moment. Walk with me."

DeAngela met Bridget's stride and shared her concerns that some of her direct reports overseeing logistics were finding one of the Seven Cornerstones of Teamwork challenging; specifically, the sharing of soft resources with some of the other areas. "Particularly with sales," concluded DeAngela.

"Have you discussed this with Gisela?"

"Yes, we are both bumping up against some of the same challenges," said DeAngela.

"Are you available to meet now?" asked Bridget.

DeAngela tapped her watch, pulling up her calendar. "I am."

"Great, see if Gisela is, too, and the two of you meet me in my office."

Nick met her at the elevator. "Good morning, Bridget. Ray and Harry are in your office, and DeAngela just messaged that Giscla will also be joining you."

"Great. Thanks, Nick."

"Good morning, gentlemen. I'm sorry I'm late."

"No worries. The extra few minutes gave Ray and me time to finalize next month's messaging," said Harry, "and Nick let us know that Gisela and DeAngela would be joining us."

"And here they are," said Bridget as she grabbed her notebook off her desk and took a seat at the conference table with the rest of the team.

Bridget walked everyone through her thoughts on supporting the Accountable Leader Loop with additional reinforcement as well as her conversation with Natasha about what it means to truly reinforce the application of behaviors in a way that assures long-term sustainability. Then she turned to Ray, "I've asked Gisela and DeAngela to be part of the meeting so we can apply what we are talking about to a real-time example."

"Perfect," said Ray, turning to Gisela and DeAngela. "Tell us what's going on."

DeAngela provided an overview of the feedback they were receiving about the sharing of ideas between logistics and sales.

"It sounds like an issue at the line manager level, not trusting that their ideas are being heard and utilized."

"I agree," said DeAngela.

"Me too," said Gisela, "but we have both been modeling, coaching, and requiring the sharing of resources with our direct reports, both hard and soft, and we're actively engaging in activities around teamwork. There must be more we can do. We're just not sure what."

"The next phase of the planned reinforcement is leader kits," said Ray. "The kits are a tool used to create weekly dialogue between the leader and their employees around targeted content. The content is focused on any number of topics like common language, tapping in, what it means to achieve ten bars of gold, and any of the cornerstones, like shared resources. I was just about to introduce them to you, so we'll start with that topic."

"Sounds very practical," said Bridget. "Moving forward, how can we reinforce for all employees that their ideas and their contributions are important and that we value them?"

Ray explained that as a team, they had already demonstrated to everyone the importance of speaking up through the tapping-in training and ongoing reinforcement. "But," he continued, "it sounds like we need to reinforce the importance of listening through to the end of what the other person has to say. It can be easy for all of us to believe we understand what is being said before the person finishes, so we tune out or cut them off, telling them, 'I know what you mean.' But too often, we don't."

Ray went on to explain that when he and his team teach listening, they show people a seven-minute video of a kernel of popcorn heating up in oil and popping, and then they instruct them to watch all the way through to the end, since initially it looks nothing like popcorn. "Otherwise they will not fully understand what they have been seeing. We call it 'popping the popcorn' because just as they had to wait to realize the kernel in oil was to become a piece of popcorn, so must we listen through the entire 'popping process' of conversation without interruption if we are to truly understand what is being said and the value of a perspective or idea.

"After the video has been viewed by their team, leaders use cards that we provide them that have questions they can use over the next few weeks. These cards will offer opportunities for a short five-minute weekly discussion together, like 'Where have you had a chance to pop the popcorn this week?' and 'Where have you missed the opportunity to pop the popcorn?' This dialogue together reinforces good listening and the value of the soft resources that people are willing to share."

"So," Gisela said, "we don't need a trainer, or a day in class—it's just a few minutes each week of purposeful dialogue between the line manager and employee about a prescribed topic?"

"That's right," said Ray.

"Effective and efficient. I love that," said DeAngela.

"Leader kits like these are just one of the tools we will use over the next several months to equip the frontline leaders to continually reinforce the application of the new behaviors everyone has been taught," Ray summed up. "This continued focus on sustaining and applying the learning, in conjunction with the Accountable Leader Loop, will ensure the people-first initiative will become part of Talon Tech's DNA."

Bridget was confident she now understood what Ray had meant by *retention* and was glad, once again, that she had made the decision to follow his advice and stay the course.

TRUST THE
PROCESS

"Good luck with your big day today," said Rob as he corralled the kids and headed out the door. Bridget stood in the doorway waving until they had pulled out of the driveway and headed down the street. She closed the door, took a deep breath, and then made a mental note of the day ahead. Walk with Natasha, farewell gathering for Ray and his team, and … "To cap off the day," she said out loud, "my keynote address on transformational leadership." Today was going to be a great day.

Just as Bridget finished lacing up her sneakers, Natasha pulled into the driveway, and Bridget stepped outside to meet her.

"Thank you for walking with me this morning," said Natasha. "I'm in need of a walk and talk."

"Glad you suggested it—the weather's too nice to be stuck in the gym rowing. Tell me what's going on."

For the first twenty minutes of the walk, Natasha outlined how her company's transformation was slowly unraveling. "As you know, we continued to be successful for several months after Ray and his team had exited, or so I thought. When I lost two of my senior leaders within a period of three months—unexpected and unrelated to the transformation, just life stuff—the cracks began to appear."

"That's rough," said Bridget.

"Yeah, it was and still is, because sections within each of their leadership spheres began to lose focus on the initiative—they just didn't stand up without those leaders leading the charge, and my HR team did not have the skills or the experience to handle the void. All that resulted in our momentum dying out." Natasha went on to explain that although they had hired replacements, those new senior leaders didn't have a united culture to immerse themselves in, so it had been a slower process getting them embedded in the initiative.

"So, what's your plan of action?"

"Well, after exiting almost a year and a half ago, Ray and his team are coming back next week."

"So," said Bridget, "today Talon Tech says goodbye to Ray and his team after two years of working with them, and next week he returns to VGS Medical! I remember when you were talking about being ready—you were, like, thirteen months in, and we were still newbies at seven months into our transformation. But when we crossed the year mark, I was tempted."

"I know, and I'm so glad you took Marty's advice instead of mine," said Natasha. "Of course, if you tell him I said that, I'll deny it. I feel guilty enough about the loss of momentum and productivity in my own company, and I definitely wouldn't want to feel guilty about having convinced you to do the same."

"You and me both," said Bridget. "As soon as we finish our walk, I have to get ready to head to the office to say goodbye to Ray and his team."

"And then," said Natasha with a smile, "I'll see you this afternoon for your keynote address on transformation—clearly, I still have lots to learn!"

When Bridget arrived at the conference room, she saw that it was set up beautifully for the gathering and that the senior leadership team had begun to arrive. Everyone agreed it was a bittersweet moment—they were ecstatic to recognize that they had achieved "India ink" and were equipped to provide the same level of ongoing support and training that Ray and his team had provided while at the same time sorry to be saying goodbye to Ray, Gloria, and Jason, who had become honorary members of the Talon Tech team.

When the guests of honor arrived, everyone clapped. Once everyone was seated, Bridget clinked her glass with her fork, quieting the room.

"Ray, I want to thank you and your team for guiding us well on our transformational journey over these past twenty-four months. We now understand the importance of behavior change, and we have reaped its benefits. Applying the behaviors solved our chip problem back in the early days of our people-first initiative. We then applied it to solve our safety issue before it could gain traction. We've modeled, coached, required, and reinforced all behaviors until they became embedded in the fabric of our culture. We couldn't have done it without your expertise and guidance. Thank you!"

"You're very welcome," said Ray. "It's been a true pleasure working with all of you!"

Congratulations and handshakes broke out among the leadership team. Then Bridget clinked her glass again.

"As we bid goodbye to Ray and his team, we have some exciting news for Talon Tech's future. I was given the opportunity several months ago to buy Smart Tech, but I felt we were not yet ready.

Today, when I look at our team, the culture we have created, and the amazing potential of our people that we have released, I know we *are* ready. The acquisition will be final next week!"

Everyone got to their feet, cheering and clapping. "Congratulations, Bridget," said Dishant.

"The congratulations belong to all of you," said Bridget, meeting the eyes of each member of her leadership team. "Together, we've come so far, and Talon Tech is now well poised to reach extraordinary heights."

When Bridget arrived at the conference later that afternoon, she was still feeling energized by the morning's events. Before heading in, she took a few moments to review her notes for the session. Initially, Bridget had planned on delivering a speech for her keynote, but then she decided what she really wanted was to make herself available for the questions of her audience—all fellow CEOs. The conference coordinators loved her idea and disseminated the overview of Talon Tech's transformation that Bridget had provided them with in advance. With that information in the hands of the attendees, the time could now be solely focused on a Q and A format.

Bridget couldn't help but smile when she saw the copies of the *Harvard Business Review*, with "Transformational Leadership" as its cover story, on display in the lobby. Being featured in *HBR* as a transformational guru had been a highlight of the journey she had traveled these past two years. Once settled in her seat on the stage, Bridget invited her colleagues to ask any and all questions that would help them on their transformational journeys.

The first question came as no surprise to Bridget: "Did you find it difficult to move from a tech mindset to a people mindset?"

"Absolutely," said Bridget. "It was one of the hardest things I've ever had to do, but fortunately I realized the importance of people and that to harness the full potential of every team member, leadership and the organization needed to adopt and embrace a people mindset *and* a tech mindset."

"What about the cost? You had to hire a consultant with a team of people to help with the transformation."

"It was a leap of faith to be sure," Bridget explained. "We had to choose to invest in our people just as we invest in facilities and technology and research against an outcome. I believed that investing in our people would pay better dividends than many of these other investments—and it most definitely did. Make no mistake, transforming an organization requires a significant investment of time, training, resources, funds, and commitment. If you don't stay the course and sort out the problems along the way, those dividends will not materialize."

"What was your measure of success when all was said and done? You've talked about employee engagement and profitability, but did you have a personal measure of success, too?"

"Great question," said Bridget. "I left one of my early board meetings convinced that if I could figure out how to harness the potential of my people, we would win. But perhaps more importantly, a personal measure of success for me was everyone on the executive team also coming to see the value in harnessing the power of our people. I knew that value needed to be embedded in the leadership, not just in me. And we achieved that. We have, of course, had our challenges along the way, but by and large, the people who remain about 97 percent retention—are fully committed ... and that's how I know Talon Tech's transformation will outlast my leadership."

The questions continued for another hour, and Bridget felt pleased that she could answer with confidence and see that her audience was clearly valuing their time together. She had certainly come a long way since that board-driven wake-up call so many months ago. Today had been a great day.

LEADING WHAT MATTERS MOST

"Good morning, everyone!" boomed Bridget.

"Good morning!" roared the room.

"I am beyond excited to have you, our newest Talon Tech members, race across the vast and perilous desert together. I hope you are feeling both rested and energized!"

"We are!" came excited shouts.

"I warn you, it's not as easy as it may appear, but the lessons and insights you will take away from this experience will fire you up! And that collective fire is what will release the full potential of every one of you!"

People began clapping. "And now I'd like to introduce you to the person who will facilitate your desert-crossing experience this morning—Talon Tech's chief financial officer, Dishant Patel!"

Cheers filled the room as Dishant jogged up to the podium.

As Bridget made her exit from the training session, she couldn't help but smile. They had done it. The people-first initiative was in Talon Tech's DNA, and they were aligning every new employee with that DNA.

Several senior leaders had volunteered to facilitate the kickoff training for all the new employees acquired from the Smart Tech acquisition, but Dishant had won out. He had, after all, been the one who'd committed right from the start, a commitment that never once faltered during their transformational journey that had led them to this point. Bridget had assured them all that there were plenty of experiential training sessions in Talon Tech's future and that they would each get their turn to facilitate. *Ha!* she thought, recalling their first leadership meeting with Ray. *Never could I have imagined that one day my senior leaders would be fighting over who gets to facilitate the training.*

As she exited the building, her watch dinged. She had to pick up her pace if she was going to be on time for her meeting with Natasha and Marty.

"Good morning," said Bridget as she took her coat off and took a seat at the table. "Did you order yet?"

"Nope—waiting for you," Marty said, waving the waiter over.

"You two go ahead. I'll decide by the time you finish ordering."

With breakfast and coffee in front of them, Marty said, "So, how's it feel, Bridget?"

Bridget paused for a moment and then raised her coffee cup. "To weathering the storm and coming out the other side." She put down her cup and looked at her friends. "Truly, I don't think I could have gotten through it without your support. Thank you, both."

"You're welcome," replied Natasha and Marty.

"Unfortunately," said Natasha, "I won't be coming out on the other side of my storm for at least another year, potentially two. And," she said, looking at Marty, "do not say I told you so."

Marty put his hand on his chest as if wounded. "I would never tell you I told you so," he said with a grin.

Bridget swatted Marty's arm. "Ray's been back three months now, right? Any progress?" she asked Natasha.

"VGS Medical's 'take two' with Ray and his team is going well in terms of being familiar to almost everyone, and there are areas in which the new behaviors really stuck. The biggest challenge is getting full buy-in from everyone … again. There are pockets of people at every level questioning the company's—and if I'm honest, my own—commitment to the transformation this time around. But," she said with a smile, "I'm confident we'll come out the other side of this stronger than ever, and today is all about celebrating Talon Tech's success!"

"Yes!" echoed Marty. "Give us the skinny on how the acquisition went and the next steps."

Bridget gave them an overview of the past three months since the official closing on the acquisition, which included equipping her team to train the new employees brought over from Smart Tech on all the people-first behaviors. "In fact," said Bridget, "we kicked it off with the Gold of the Desert Kings training just this morning.

"These past few months have been a whirlwind to be sure," she continued. "I think Rob and the kids were starting to forget what I looked like. But now that our people-first culture is fully embedded in the organization and the acquisition is complete, my work-life balance is back in sync and—also great news—every metric, from customer and employee satisfaction and retention to productivity and profitability, continues to soar."

Bridget took a sip of her coffee and leaned in conspiratorially. "So, after my *HBR* article and my keynote Q and A, I've been approached by a couple of agents to write a book about my transformational leadership. Is that crazy?"

"That's incredible!" said Natasha, clapping her hands.

"That's fantastic news, Bridget," Marty said, beaming.

"Really?"

"Yes!" they both said in unison.

"Rob thinks it is, too. I'm going to do it," said Bridget, laughing.

That evening after dinner, Bridget sat in the quiet of her study listening to Rob help the kids with their homework before sending them off to bed. As her Transformation Notebook, now completely full, lay open in front of her, Bridget reached into her bag and pulled out a new notebook and scrawled *Transformational Leadership Book* across its cover.

Taking a breath, she exhaled and began to write.

Book Outline

1. Lead + Train + Implement + Practice = Success

Embed a people-first culture in the fabric of the organization by doing the following:

- *Recognize that leadership behaviors and employee behaviors need to be different from what they currently are. It's not about different HR policies and procedures.*

- *Equip all leaders to demonstrate "true" leadership that allows and encourages people to perform to their full potential:*

  - *Encourage input into decisions.*

  - *Provide additional new tools and skills to help them do their job brilliantly.*

- *Consistently communicate the people-first initiative to all employees. Let them know where Talon Tech is going with respect to enabling them to contribute to their full potential and their importance to our future by doing the following:*

- *Define this priority and stick to it.*

      □ *Reference this initiative in regular staff meetings and company-wide town halls.*

      □ *Ensure employee objectives and reviews reflect this initiative.*

- *Provide training and practice.*

2. Remember the Six Areas of Focus

- *Leadership: Each of us must own the outcome for this initiative and hold people accountable for modeling the new behaviors.*

- *Communication: Let everyone know continually and consistently how we are doing things and why. This must be intentional and planned for.*

- *Alignment: Align all the human resource practices. This shift in how we're leading our people must touch every aspect of what HR is responsible for.*

- *Training: Use experiential training. First train leaders at all levels, then train all employees. Be sure the training links to our real-world issues.*

- *Reinforcement: Provide support and activities to ensure that the training sticks. These must be led by our line managers.*

- *Metrics: Continuous measurement of progress/outcomes. Share these with everyone.*

3. Ten Bars of Gold Every Time

- *Know and get agreement on what ten bars of gold looks like for all major objectives.*

- *Take time to gather all available information and plan to achieve all that's possible.*

- *Use all team members' insight and skill.*

- *Deal with the unknown head on: don't avoid it.*

As CEO, remember the following:
- *The power of investing in everyone:*
    - *Common language*
    - *Common understanding*
    - *Respect for every individual regardless of rank*
- *The positive impact of our senior leaders setting the pace by example.*
- *Don't confuse early wins with ultimate success. Stay the course!*
- *The importance of giving the whole team the full picture of our two-year plan.*

4. Changing Behaviors Requires Consistency and Time

- *Trust the process.*
- *Support the decision-making process.*
- *Training is best when tailored to real-time issues.*

5. The Seven Cornerstones of Teamwork

- *Leadership—black*
- *Unanimous Focus on a Common Goal—green*
- *Clearly Defined Roles for Subgroups—light blue*
- *Shared Resources—yellow*
- *Effective and Frequent Communication—purple*
- *Consistent, United, and Enthusiastic Effort—dark blue*
- *Periodic and Temporary Suppression of the Ego—red*

6. It's Not Magic: The Process Is Foolproof If You Follow It

- *Our executives are trained to model, coach, and require the new behavior.*

- *Our leaders are trained to model, coach, and require the new behavior.*

- *Our employees are trained on the new behavior and understand that their leader is there to coach them on those behaviors.*

- *We employ the Accountable Leader Loop consistently:*

  □ *Commit to putting the new behaviors into practice in every applicable circumstance.*

  □ *Test it regularly to make sure the loop is reaching every level.*

- *Line managers are equipped to sustain, reinforce, and help apply the new behaviors on the job until they are part of Talon Tech's DNA.*

- *Our human resources processes and policies are tied to our people-first initiative:*

  □ *We promote people who demonstrate the new behavior.*

  □ *We hire people who have an inclination toward the new behavior.*

- *All our communications reinforce that the new behavior is the way to go.*

- *We share our metrics that result from consistently practicing the new behavior.*

- *If we consistently and continually follow this process, we will achieve ten bars of gold every time.*

As Bridget finished her last note, her phone buzzed. It was a text from Jordan: *Just an FYI, we've run into a mechanical glitch in our Oklahoma manufacturing facility, but my team and I have it covered.*

Bridget texted back, *I know you do!*

ABOUT THE AUTHOR

Phil Geldart, founder and CEO of Eagle's Flight, is a recognized authority in the areas of transforming organizational culture, leadership development, and experiential learning solutions. His passion for releasing human potential has fueled many innovative programs that have garnered the trust and respect of top Fortune 500 global organizations.

Phil pioneered experiential learning in the training and development industry over thirty years ago, and today, Eagle's Flight is an industry leader whose experiential learning programs have been translated into more than two dozen languages and sold to teams around the world.

An inspirational speaker and author, Phil shares his expertise with audiences and readers alike in areas crucial to performance improvement.

ACKNOWLEDGMENTS

A particular thanks to Beth Cooper for her outstanding help in bringing this book to fruition. Without her superpower ability to both understand the complexities of changing human behavior and then the skill to capture that understanding in a compelling manner, this book would never have seen the light of day. Thank you, Beth, for your patience and brilliance.

Thanks also to the outstanding team at Advantage Media and Forbes Books, whose consistent professionalism and support has been with me from the beginning, immensely valuable, and greatly appreciated.

CONTACT

If you're interested in harnessing the full potential of each individual within your organization, you can find out more about Phil Geldart and Eagle's Flight at philgeldart.com.